HUNTING
THE SOUTHERN TRADITION

HUNTING
THE SOUTHERN TRADITION

MAY LAMAR & RICH DONNELL

PHOTOGRAPHY BY CHIP COOPER

TAYLOR PUBLISHING COMPANY
DALLAS, TEXAS

Library of Congress Cataloging-in-Publication Data

Donnell, Rich.
    Hunting: the Southern tradition/Rich Donnell and May Lamar;
photography by Chip Cooper.
    ISBN 0-87833-536-6
    1. Hunting—Social aspects—Southern States. 2. Hunting—Southern
States. 3. Southern States—Social life and customs. I. Lamar, May.
II. Cooper, Chip. III. Title.
SK43.D63 1987
799.2975—dc19

Printed in the United States of America

0   9   8   7   6   5

An Atticus Press Book

Book Design: Constance Flowers

ACKNOWLEDGMENTS

We gratefully acknowledge the help and hospitality of the many people who helped make this book possible: Dr. Everett Hale, Bob and Robert Almon, Tom Atkinson and the Wheeler National Game Refuge, Forrest Bailey, Cook's Bend Hunting Club; Harriet, Liza, and Brandon Cooper; King Curry and the Millwood Hunting Club, DCH Rabbit Hunters, Keith Dismukes, Dixie Hunting Club, Melvin Dukes, Wayne Fears, Hilliard Fletcher, The Cook Brothers, Jex Luce, Tombigbee Teal Club, Robert Leigh, Ben Kelly Strain, Dr. Bud Cardinal, Jim Kirby, C.C. Davis, John Hardin, Jack Leigh, Dr. Joab Thomas, Mike Ellis, Jimmy Hinton Jr., Jimmy Hinton Sr., Dr. Doug Jones, Charles Kelly and crew, Tom Kelly, Dr. Woodie Lamar, Tommy Latham, Will Lett, Jefferson Hunting Club, Ben Radcliff, Man Rand, Dr. Larry Skelton and the Moundville Coon Hunters; Ben, Billy, and Dut Stimpson, and sons; Tennessee Valley Coon Dog Hunter's Association, Brady Weaver, Judge George Wright, and a special thanks to Bobby Frese for making this thing fly.

Authors' and Photographer's Note: The photographs used with the text do not necessarily relate directly to the people or places being discussed but rather are used generally to evoke and reinforce the atmosphere and sensations of hunting and the southern tradition.

Table of Contents

THE LAND 1

THE EQUIPMENT 65

THE DOGS 113

THE HUNTER 151

THE LAND

A boy raised on family land in the deep South is a fortunate boy. From his elders, he learns how to bait hooks and catch fish. He learns what to use a rifle and a shotgun for, and he learns how to shoot. He learns the terrain and the species on it, and he learns how to hunt. He learns how to clean game, what tastes good and what doesn't. As he practices the skills of a sportsman, he finds himself pausing with his elders to appreciate land's network.

He hears the great horned owl at dawn.

He watches a storm on a small pond.

He sees the silhouette of ducks flying overhead.

He hushes at the gracefulness of a doe.

He studies the faint outline of the foothills through an evening mist.

He senses a change in the weather, and watches it happen.

As the boy becomes a young man he experiences these intricacies of land over and over again. They're there. He hears them. He sees them. He smells them. He touches them. He tastes them. He experiences the elements of truth as he grows to understand the interaction of wildlife, plantlife, and the seasons. He believes in a God who has crafted this natural masterpiece. He becomes responsible to the land.

His commitment brings moments of unrest. He hears of a nearby
landowner who has sold a great portion of his acreage to a corporation.
He hears of another landowner leasing hunting rights to his land to
men from outside the area. He worries not only about these families giving
up their land, but about local acquaintances who have now lost access
to that land. He worries that those with little access will excuse themselves for trespassing and poaching, a problem already inflammed
by the criminal element, as when poachers dump their dogs to run bucks,
tattering the reputation of sincere dog hunters while slicing into the
well-being of all wildlife. He worries whether government will replenish its
conservation chest, raising the funds necessary to maintain what few
public game management areas remain. But these concerns impress
upon him the preciousness of his land and he vows to pass this land and

an understanding of his obligation to it–having been so educated by his father and uncle and grandfather–along to his son and nephew and grandson.

More often than not in the deep South, the son and nephew and grandson have inherited the family business as well as the land. The success of that business probably enabled the family to acquire much of its land. Frequently, that business is lumber. An aesthetic and practical appreciation for the natural resource—the forest—is what links the family's love of land and lumber.

The traditional portrait of the lumberman as a hard-working, strong-willed man, the epitome of individualism, remains accurate today. Ben Stimpson is such a lumberman, as are his brothers Billy and Gordon and their sons. Their individualism evolves from a strong family unit. Locals seldom refer to any one Stimpson; rather it's "The Stimpsons."

The Stimpsons own and operate Gulf Lumber Company on the outskirts of downtown Mobile. Ben Stimpson speaks above the whine from behind his office desk about the problems confronting the Southern lumberman. A big man with white hair, drooping eyes, and strong nose, Stimpson speaks with an impressive drawl. A very natural, confident, deep drawl. The kind of drawl a film director should study if he intends to portray a gentleman of the deep South. Stimpson's words hang long enough to touch each other even when he's thinking of what to say next; just when a word is about to expire after a slow slide back down his throat, another word crawls over it.

Stimpson speaks of Gulf Lumber's ongoing multimillion-dollar sawmill renovation. It is a project many lumber operations in the country, at least those who can afford it, are having to undertake to get more lumber out of a log. To do that, less is being left to the eyesight and judgement of the man operating the saw, the sawyer. There are actually instruments out there that will electronically scan or read the shape of a log to determine exactly how many one inch and two inch thick pieces of lumber are in that log. A picture of the log, showing where these pieces are, will appear on a video monitor. And the computerized machinery will automatically adjust and saw those pre-designated number of one and two inch pieces out of the log. The sawing process gets much more involved, and varies with each mill, but the point is that high technology has come to the lumber business. No wonder Stimpson says of his family's battle with modernization, "It's the devil. It costs like the dickens." Stimpson shakes his head and sighs, "If a fellow had what it takes to get in the business today and build a sawmill, he wouldn't want to."

Unfortunately, the Stimpsons and many other Southern lumbermen not only have to tangle with the task of building and operating a modern mill, they must also confront a major problem stemming from the increased production this same advanced technology will allow them. Ask any Southern landowner about the lumber coming into the region from Canada that is underpricing their lumber and consuming a third of their market. How, one might reasonably ask, can Canadian lumbermen pay for processing lumber, ship it South, and *still charge less than the local family operation down the road*? United States lumbermen say Canada's government charges its forest products companies an extremely low fee for purchasing government-owned trees that are to be cut down and processed into lumber, just so those companies can gain a healthy share of the U.S. market. Canadian lumbermen counter that their increasing market share is because of an appreciation of the U.S. dollar relative to the Canadian dollar, because its production costs are lower, and perhaps because U.S. builders prefer Canada's spruce-pine-fir species to Southern Yellow Pine. Ben Stimpson is hopeful a recent compromise in which Canada will impose a 15% export tax on its U.S. bound lumber that will at least slow down the Canadian influx. "If they don't do something a lot of mills are going to be put out of business," Stimpson says. "We can't compete with the Canadian government. There's no question about what they're doing."

Such is the life of a Southern lumberman. But the lumberman can escape, really escape, from these mounting pressures at the sawmill; for not only did Fred Stimpson and others like him put lumber in their sons' respective futures, they also led them to some of the finest land in the deepest woods of the South. A good chunk of that acreage lies in Clarke County at Choctaw Bluff, north of the junction of the Tombigbee and Alabama Rivers. The family's country home, built by Fred Stimpson, sits just off the Alabama River and was the site of a Confederate garrison, Fort Stonewall, which protected the area's rich salt springs and blocked any Yankee ships from moving upstream to the Rebel arsenal and navy yard located northward on the river at Selma. The principal remnant from the fort is a cannon facing the river, mounted directly in front of the house.

The Stimpsons maintain an exclusive hunting compound at Choctaw Bluff. Membership includes some of the oldest names and oldest money in the area. The Stimpsons also have hunting rights to thousands of

acres in Washington County, west of Choctaw Bluff. They refer to it as
Bullpen. Most every serious Southern hunter knows of Bullpen and of the
ripe and diverse game living off the vast, plush forest along the Tombigbee River. The Stimpsons and their very, very close friends hunt both
Choctaw Bluff and Bullpen.

"My father and Jim Radcliff were hunting buddies," Ben Stimpson

says. "They were leasing land and what have you. They recognized that if they were going to have a place to hunt they would have to acquire it somehow. They realized they could buy this Bullpen tract, so they were getting a group together to buy it. Just on account of hunting. In the process my father ran into a friend of his named Ben May. He's dead now. He didn't hunt or fish. Ben May made a lot of money exporting lumber

to England during World War I. He was looking for some good investments in timberland and Daddy showed him that the land would be a damn good investment timberwise. They made a deal that Mr. May would buy the land and let them have the hunting." That was in the early 1920s. The land at Bullpen, the core of it, says Ben Stimpson, still belongs to the Ben May Charitable Foundation.

Fred Stimpson later encouraged Ben May to invest in a few thousand acres at Choctaw Bluff. Fred Stimpson eventually bought back most of that land from Ben May and the Stimpsons have added to it through the years.

The Stimpsons treat their land royally with a sincere obligation to game conservation. "The Harold family and the Slade family at Sunflower were the first to really start a program of game management in the southeast," Stimpson says. "They saw that if you treated the game right, the game would come back. My father and Mr. Radcliff saw what they were doing and copied them. My father and Mr.

Radcliff realized they had to quit being game hogs. My father killed 96 turkeys one year and Mr. Radcliff killed 94. They recognized they had to change their ways."

They did change their ways. Fred Stimpson helped to found, serving as its first president, the Alabama Wildlife Federation, and was named the state's conservationist of the year. He spearheaded the establishment of research programs, the creation of refuges and sanctuaries, and the initiation of game reestablishment projects. Turkey and deer populations began to blossom thanks to government stocking efforts that relied on sanctuaries like Fred Stimpson's as a source for game. "Long ago at Choctaw Bluff you rarely saw a deer," Ben Stimpson says. "In fact they found a half an antler one time and it was such an oddity they had it mounted."

Today, the Stimpsons continue to work closely with the state's conservation people. Two ongoing programs include shooting doe to ward off overpopulation and shooting the smaller bucks while sparing the big ones in order to promote bigger horned bucks. Ben Stimpson says it is the family's tradition of game and land conservation he so proudly values as a Southerner. He trusts the family will continue it. One thing is for certain, the Stimpsons have ample land to work with. Land which Ben Stimpson says gives him a feeling that's difficult to describe. "It's the country," he says. "There's just something about the country. There's a sense of satisfaction."

"Highways have made it a lot more accessible," says Mister Ben, who is a buddy of Ben Stimpson's. "When I was a child everybody worked until noon Saturday. We'd leave home after work and come up here to the country by automobile. There were no four-wheel drives then. It would take several hours to go a distance that now takes 50 minutes. We wouldn't get up there till dark. Sunday morning we'd be up early, hunt all day, turn around and get back home at midnight. It was a tough damn way to hunt."

Satisfaction. Watch it seep into Mister Ben's soul as he heads into the country. He becomes a different man, a better man, the deeper into the wilderness he gets. The spirit of the land pushes the everyday problems of 20th century manhood from his weary head. The spirit cleanses him. He is rejuvenated.

About 20 miles after having passed through Calvert, where during those days when Mister Ben says it was a tough damn way to hunt the paved road had actually ended at Joe Nader's store, Mister Ben now turns his four-wheel pickup off the highway onto a dirt track and steers far into a river bottom hardwood forest. Rich oaks, gums, and cypress shadow swamps that appear to be painted deep green. Blending into invisibility throughout this site are scrumptious numbers of deer, turkey, squirrel, rabbits, hogs, and ducks. "This road we're on, when the river's up you can run an outboard motor right down the middle of it."

But on this November afternoon, a month before the rains will drain south, as they do each year, forcing the Tombigbee to rise, Mister Ben's battered rig handles the terrain nonchalantly as it escorts him into the wild. His eyes grow wide and alert. His hefty frame perks toward the wheel. He points to a curious doe. He fingers his pistol upon spotting a

hurried sow. He cusses the beaver for the death it has inflicted on a stand of hardwoods. He says this area, Washington County, and nearby Clarke and Wilcox Counties, held most of what few turkeys roamed the southeast during the early decades of the century, and that local turkeys were stocked in the state's northern counties and some were even transplanted into Northern states such as Michigan. Mister Ben says turkey is his favorite game and that he killed his first at age six. "When I was younger, I hunted hard. Now I enjoy just as much watching the game and being out here and fooling around with things."

The dirt road winds endlessly into the wilderness. Leaves fall and settle on the surface of a swamp. A rabbit bounds by. Crows in flight talk amongst themselves. Suddenly a breeze carries in the aroma of river, a clean river smell; it shoots into the nostrils and charges the entire body. This is the heart of the country. And up ahead a house becomes visible through the forest. It is a long, wooden, single-story structure overlooking a bend in the river. Mister Ben pulls around back and parks amid a half-dozen other pickups. Nearby, the owners of those trucks hover over two dressed boars and a sow about to be tucked in the outdoor freezer that two men are scrubbing down. The hunters, young and old, glance Mister Ben's way.

Had Mister Ben been somebody other than Mister Ben, the hunters would have resumed their conversation and acknowledged the newcomer only when their story ceased. In the South, a person does not simply walk up and take control, whether it's on the porch of a general store, around the engine of a broken down chevy, or standing over dead hogs in the woods; that is, unless a person is special, unless he is someone like Mister Ben, one of the older members, whose daddy hunted with Fred Stimpson, whose daddy along with Fred Stimpson founded the Bullpen. And so when the hunters see Mister Ben approaching they do not carry on. They halt their conversation and open up the circle. The older hunters greet Mister Ben first, then the younger ones. He walks through the group and gazes down at the game. The sow displays a giant hole in its side. A younger man courageously speaks up. "Mister Ben, this sow looks like it was shot with a Russian-launched missile," he drawls, chuckling along with the others, including Mister Ben, until Mister Ben quiets, looks back down at the game and says, "What it was was a bad shot." He heads for the house. The group of men glance from Mister Ben to the messy sow and begin nodding and mumbling their agreement with Mister Ben's observation. It was a bad shot.

The house is headquarters for the Bullpen Hunting Club. The clubhouse is functional. There is no wife's touch here. Two dozen beds occupy the front and back rooms. A tiny bar with several bottles of liquor on it stands in the corner. One of the rules of the house reads: "A drink is allowed, but nip-nip-nipping all day long is frowned upon." These are reasonable men. Old hunting photos adorn the walls; some are framed, others are merely tacked up, yellowing. Mister Ben pauses in front of a photo of his father and smiles.

Mister Ben feels good as he pulls out a map of the Bullpen land, spreads it across a table and loses himself in the vast acreage. It is the same land his father hunted with Fred Stimpson; it is the land Mister Ben now hunts with Fred Stimpson's sons, and the land Mister Ben's son hunts with the Stimpson sons. Later in the morning, when it's time to go home, his other home, he pauses before he gets in his truck, looks around at the river and the house and the forest and says, "There's no place like it in the world."

Except for the next man's land in another part of the South. One would be hard-pressed to convince any Southern landowner from Mississippi to North Carolina that there is any land so fine as that beneath his feet. And if an impetuous soul really wanted to argue the point with him . . . well, as Gerald O'Hara said, "Tis the only thing worth fighting for."

On a clear, hot day in January, on very old land, two dozen hunters surround a huntmaster preparing to paddle the only man to kill a buck during the last dog drive of the season. Fred, the accused, a plump gentleman with reddening face, is shaking his head in disbelief. "Hell, I killed the damn thing," Fred says. "I ain't got to get my ass whipped." Fred receives no character defense from the jovial onlookers.

"You got off your stand, that's your trouble," replies the huntmaster, a pencil thin veteran holding a southern pine 2×4 like a baseball bat. "I was getting ready to shoot that deer myself. Now bend over."

"But he was coming from you," Fred pleads, bending. "He must have smelled you and come back toward me."

The smack of the 2×4 entertaining Fred's rear, followed by Fred's holler, draws a round of laughter. A tall man in the circle asks no one in particular, "I wonder how many men have felt the paddle here through the years?" An answer floats from the group. "Probably a whole damn lot."

Probably so, considering a hunting camp has survived for over 100 years at Millwood, which is the name of this 3,500 acre plot along the Black

Warrior River. The man who asked the question, the tall man with strong eyes and graying hair, is Judge George Wright. He owns Millwood, though he'll deny it. "Like the old saying goes, I don't own the land, the land owns me," Judge Wright will say. "All we're doing on this earth is holding it for a little period of time. While we're here we've got to see what we can do to help it."

A while later, while sipping a bloody mary and eating venison in the lunch room of the hunting lodge, Judge Wright tells the story of Millwood. In the 1820s a man named Robert Withers, a doctor and planter, bought several tracts of land from the French, land originally granted to Napoleonic refugees in 1817. Withers rode from Virginia and settled with his slaves on the eastern bank of the Black Warrior. He built and operated a grist mill, a wheat mill, a steam sawmill and ginned cotton. He relied on artesian well power. Water flowed from seven wells through a brick lined canal and onto a turbine wheel that drove the machinery. Withers shipped produce downriver to Mobile. He developed Millwood into an important river landing. He built two 2-story cypress-clad structures overlooking the water, one an Inn for steamboat travelers, the other to house slaves.

After Withers died in 1854, Millwood passed through several names, including Watt, Vandegraaf, Drake, Sheppard, and Inge. In 1882, Wiley C. Tunstall, Judge Wright's great-grandfather, bought Millwood and started the hunting camp. Numerous Tunstalls held title to Millwood through the years until Judge Wright and his sister, Camille Cook, and other nieces and nephews drew for it and several other family parcels in 1964. An ace, deuce, three, and four of spades corresponded to the various plots. Judge Wright and his sister drew the four of spades and inherited Millwood. The Judge was no stranger to the land. He hunted it as a boy with his great uncle Alfred Tunstall, a former state speaker of the House, and killed his first buck on it at age 11 in 1936.

The four of spades gave Judge Wright and his sister 2,000 acres. They've added another 1,500. They balance game and timber management, overseeing plentiful numbers of deer, turkey, and duck, 2,000 acres of river bottom hardwoods, and 1,000 acres of pine along the sandy ridges.

Walking into the front room of the clubhouse, which was the old Inn, presently undergoing restoration along with the former slave quarters, Judge Wright encounters a friend sitting in an easy chair telling another hunter one of the many old stories. A judge by the name of James Hobson, father of the late Spanish-American War hero, Admiral Richmond Pearson Hobson, traveled to Millwood to escape the yellow fever plague in Greensboro. Folks here stuck Hobson in a closet under the stairs in the old Inn to fumigate him with a sulphur candle so he wouldn't expose others to the fever. He was left in the closet a lengthy period. When he was finally released from his dreary confinement, the irritated judge bellowed: "If that is Southern hospitality, damn it, I'd rather have the yellow fever!"

Judge Wright, the storyteller, and the listener collaborate on a good chuckle. One wonders how many men have told and heard that tale through the years. Probably a whole damn lot. It is said that if a person stands in the same closet during a full moon, that person will hear Hobson's anxious proclamation.

Standing in front of the stone fireplace and near the tattered plaster wall bearing century-old scribbled names and dates of kills, including G.S. Wright's in 1936, the Judge says, "I love Millwood. I truly do. I love the old stories and the old houses and the land and the hunting. Sure it's a chore to maintain. You're constantly putting time, energy and money into it, but it's well worth it. I would like to see the tradition continued. This is something you just don't let go of."

The Hunt

As Doug Jones and several hunting companions step through the cold early morning darkness their mood sparkles with nervous intensity. They are not the same men who sat leisurely about the fireplace and exchanged tales the previous evening. They say good morning to the aura of death. Their sense of matching wits and skills against the creature's desire to stay alive is crystal clear. Their spirit thirsts for competition and challenge. They understand the risks. Today, they prey as humans have preyed since the beginning. Such is the nature of the beast.

Doug Jones and these men are duck hunters. The 100-yard stretch of dirt road they walk leads to an 11-acre pond. The pond's sole purpose is to attract ducks. It is manicured with high gear and acorn trees. The ducks these men hope to kill this morning are currently contemplating rising from the nearby refuge on the Tennessee River. When they decide it's time to eat they'll take off and if they encounter a strong wind and spot Doug Jones' decoys they will come on in, welcoming the opportunity to settle in a quiet area.

"Generally there's a very wary hen in each flock," Doug Jones says. "And boy she will really watch. They'll circle and they'll circle and if they see anything, just a little bit of a red shirt, they'll flare just like that."

Doug Jones knows this because he has hunted duck all of his life. His father, Walter Jones, put this pond together. When the men sat around the fire not too many hours ago, Doug Jones revealed his first and greatest mistake as a duck hunter at the age of 16 on the Mobile Delta.

"I didn't have much sense then," he says. "I saw ducks on the water a mile off. I was facing forward so I could watch while I rowed. Just when I reached down for my gun a guy in this blind coughs politely and I see my ducks, a big stool of decoys in front of me. There was no way to hide. Life's longest minute."

A handsome man with a day's growth of whiskers, which he won't shave until he's ready to leave the family clubhouse here and return to civilization, Jones offers in a nutshell his reasons for his love of duck hunting.

"I think it's probably the most companionable thing that I do," he says. "It gives me a chance to get away from the pressures of my job. Then there's this thing of pitting yourself against the elements, of getting out there and setting the decoys and breaking the ice. It gives you a sense of working for it. I think it's also the excitement in shooting well and being able to display your skills. No hunter likes to miss, it's tacky."

Jones says the prettiest sight in the world is watching a flock decide to set and then after a controlled drop locking their wings just above the water. If he and these men have their way today, that will be the ducks' final act.

A moment later Jones prepares a path to the blinds in the pond by beating and breaking frozen ice with a stick. This is no easy task. He is, as he says, working for it. Eventually the ice parts and the pond becomes a chorus of chimes as the other hunters move carefully out into it. Their waders protect them from the water which rises to their thighs. The arena's silver tint is breathtaking.

As the dawn breaks, the men hide themselves and wait. Two men sit in a blind to-ward the middle of the pond. Two others stand behind the brush just outside the pond. Three men, including Doug Jones, stand in the ice using the oak trees as cover. Flocks of geese and duck are visible in the distant sky where an ornery front builds. And then several mallards fly high over the pond. Jones blows his call to coerce them to circle back, but they pass. Another group approaches and passes, but this time they do circle back and two mallards dip toward the water. A susie is shot down by one of the men standing in the water behind an oak. That man will later say that ever since he learned mallards mate for life he can't help but feel deeply when he shoots one down, knowing its companion is flying about alone.

A minute later a single woody finds the site inviting and hovers in. A shot misses and it flutters away. Jones quacks an ugly nasal response at the man in the blind who missed. Missing is tacky. The man who fired shakes his head with disappointment and embarrassment. His error does not go unnoticed by any of the participants in this semi-circle setup. Unlike many other forms of hunting, duck hunters can see how every-body else is doing. Shooting is the name of the game and if a fella in a three-piece suit can shoot he will obtain a position of respect. If he can shoot it doesn't matter how unlike a model hunter he is.

The ducks are not coming in in the numbers the hunters hoped, and time is running out. There is some moaning and groaning. It is easy for hunters to sit on the porch and say that the kill is not particularly high on their list of reasons for hunting, but take the kill away and a great bitter taste forms in the mouth. A hole of dissatisfaction en-larges in the stomach. The walk back to camp is not long, but its length triples when no dead game is squeezed by the hunter's hand. These men did not come out here to watch ducks. They did not sleep in a room full of other men, rise before sunlight, bury themselves in warm clothing and plow through frozen ice with a shotgun over their shoulders to be satisfied with driving back to their homes and telling their friends the hunting party killed one duck, but the scenery was great.

Suddenly a dozen mallards turn toward the pond. Jones gives them an award-winning call. The mallards spot the decoys and drop down slowly, setting their wings just above the ice like a beautiful painting, just like Doug Jones described. "Now!" Jones hollers. Hunters rise from behind their blinds and step from behind trees and blast away. The ambush does not last long. Four mallards lie on the ice about the decoys. A black labrador tries to decide which one to carry home first. The men remain silent as they study the scene. The tremendous exhilaration at the moment of the kill subsides with the smoke. The chorus of icey chimes plays a subtle tune of fruition.

Land, precious land. Unfortunately, there's only so much of it. Man builds a highway and a shopping mall and there's less. Man has built a lot of highways and malls lately. He hasn't produced any more land. That realization continues to hit hard in the Southern hunting community. Particularly in the past 25 years, many large landowners have had to ask themselves if they could afford to farm their land and compete in the marketplace. Many landowners have asked themselves if they should rather sell hunting leases to supplement their income. A decreasing amount of available land and an increasing number of hunters means the value of hunting land is skyrocketing. Those that have leased their land for hunting, and even those who haven't, have tightened their boundaries to protect game.

Gone are the days of open hunting, when a man could have the run of the county, cutting across other landowners' terrain and never crossing the track of another hunter. Today a man either owns the land he hunts on, pays to belong to a private club leasing somebody else's land, or hunts with the general public on timber company land or the state's game management land. But the situation is not so cut and dry. Old attitudes, habits, and values come into play. For the non-landowner who once had access to local land, who once felt that great sense of satisfaction when he walked the land, who experienced those intricacies of land over and over again, the abrupt condition that he no longer has a local piece of acreage to roam can be absolutely horrifying. H.B., a 45-year-old man living at the western edge of the Black Belt, is such a victim of these changing times.

On a Sunday morning in late December, H.B. is chopping wood behind his tiny three-room house in the country. Smoke pours out of his chimney. His two children, a boy 12 and a girl 10, ride their bikes up and down the road in front of the house. Their voices liven the thick, cold air. H.B.'s wife, a pretty woman with her blonde hair pinned up for housework, sweeps dust out the back door and into the yard. A rusted swing-set rocks slowly with the breeze. Tractor parts, fluid cans, tools, and rags clutter an old wooden garage. An aging dog naps in the back of a severely bruised Blazer.

H.B. is a small, thin man. His face is the face of a man who makes his living outdoors. The skin is rough and grayish, slightly wrinkled about the eyes. His dark eyes peer intensely below heavy eyebrows. Thin sideburns travel the length of his ears and wind like a river back below them. As he buries his axe into a log his lips tighten with a slight snarl causing his nose to flatten and his chin to stick out. His left cheek bulges with chewing tobacco. He wears a black hat with a yellow Franklin logo on it. Franklin makes logging equipment, skidders in particular. H.B. doesn't drive a skidder, but he is a member of a six-man logging crew. He's the mainte-nance man, and has been for 25 years. He's torn down and put back together many a skidder and feller-buncher and loader and anything else that moves on a logging job. The strong lean-fingered hands he now grips his axe with are his bread and butter. After he completes his chore at the woodpile, he'll drive his truck to the shop and call on those hands to

do a little preventive maintenance on a knuckleboom loader. But H.B. shouldn't be going to the shop today. He should be in the woods stalking deer. Up until two years ago that's where he would be at this hour every Sunday morning during deer season. That was the year Mr. White died, and that was the year H.B. lost his place to hunt.

Mr. White owned 20,000 acres about 20 minutes from H.B.'s home. For years, Mr. White allowed H.B.'s daddy and a few other local acquaintances to hunt there. H.B.'s daddy, like H.B., was a maintenance whiz for a logging operation. He heard by word of mouth that Mr. White needed a man to help with about anything that required the use of a man's hands. H.B.'s daddy contacted Mr. White and they established a relationship. For the right to hunt on Mr. White's land, H.B.'s daddy built Mr. White's fences and changed Mr. White's fan belts and handled everything in between. It was a good arrangement that both men carefully cultivated.

H.B. grew up within this relationship and as a youngster accompanied his father to Mr. White's place both to hunt and to lend a helping hand. When H.B.'s father died 15 years go, H.B. inherited the relationship so to speak. Then two years ago, without a hint of a medical problem, Mr. White was felled in his backyard by a heart attack and died at age 76. Mr. White's wife had passed away several years before. He had two daughters, one who lived down on the Gulf and another who had moved to Tennessee. The daughters decided to sell a big chunk of the land to farming interests and lease the remainder for hunting rights. A group of professionals from the northern part of the state paid a handsome fee and acquired those rights.

"You start takin' things for granted and they're gone," H.B. drawls, snapping his finger. He spits wide of the wood pile and wipes his face and mouth with a blue bandanna. "Hell, after Mr. White died I knew what was gonna happen. It'd been happenin' everywhere else. I thought about gettin' some men together and tryin' to lease a piece of Mr. White's land, but at that time the mills weren't takin' many trees and our crew was down three or four days out of the week. The money just wasn't there. Not that it mattered. If I'd had it it wouldn't have been as much as them people in there now are payin'. I've kicked around the idea of joinin' a club not too far from here that has some pretty good huntin', but there're some people in it I don't care to hunt with. I mean they aren't very safe."

H.B. sits on the woodpile and hollers for his boy to come and haul the logs inside. He removes his cap and scratches his thinning black hair. He shakes his head. "It's real disappointin'. Huntin' Mr. White's land had always been what we did. It was in our blood, you know what I mean. My boy even went out there with me a couple times before Mr. White died. I ain't angry at anybody in particular. I can't blame the people who own the land for wantin' to make money off it. It's their land. I can't blame the people payin' for the right to hunt it, just cause I can't afford to. All I know is I miss bein' able to jump in my truck and be huntin' that land in 20-25 minutes."

H.B.'s boy speeds around the side of the house on his bike and slides to a stop, leading with his back wheel and shooting dirt on H.B.'s old leather boots. H.B. looks the boy over and grins. The boy smiles back and shows a mouth full of teeth, which is about the only difference in their looks. "Hell," H.B. says, "I guess when it gets right down to it, my biggest mistake has been not makin' enough money to buy my own land." H.B. pauses and rubs his chin. "I don't know, maybe I oughta go ahead and join that club, not for my sake but for the boy's sake. When I think back to my best times as a boy I was always doin' somethin' outdoors. Be a shame if my boy didn't have the same opportunity."

The old black man in the country knows something about access to land, too. The old black man will say there are not as many black people living in the country today as when all the colored people were share-croppers. The old black man knows this because he was the son of a sharecropper. He quit school in third grade because his father needed him in the field. Back then, everybody quit school. The old black man will say these things to anybody who wants to hear about the way it was from someone who was there. He isn't hard to find. Just go to the thick of Black Belt country and ask where Cotton Valley is. If nobody has heard of it, ask for Bethlehem because that's what Cotton Valley was called long ago. The old black man lives in Cotton Valley, down the dirt road, just

past the church. He lives in a modest brick home on seven acres. Two
goats, a rooster, and several hens loiter about his land. An old John Deere
tractor rests beneath a tree. A leaning wooden crop locker holds ears
of corn from his small plot. Chances are, if it's not hunting season, the old
black man will be piddling in his yard. If it is hunting season, be prepared
to wait.

He looks good for his age. He stands over six feet tall and he stands very
straight. His curled salt and pepper hair is cut close to his head. He has
a protruding chin and a flat nose. He hides his eyes with sunglasses and
covers his head with a green hunting hat. He prefers to talk as he leans
across the hood of his pickup. His words walk patiently out of his mouth.

"Back then, the black man worked for the white man. The white man loaned us some money for the plow and we'd have somebody tellin' us what to do. Back then, we farmed with a one-half-row plow and a mule. We raised 10 or 15 acres, maybe two or three bales of cotton, made our corn and peas, there was plenty of stuff to live on like that. But cotton was the money crop. On up to 1940 people was row croppin' in this country. After that, the mule went out and that shut the door on a lot of little people. Roosevelt came in and went to payin' people not to plant so much;

that's when they cut the acres down. That's what we called it, cuttin' the acres down. But when he cut 'em down to so little, the man who had a tractor could farm all that. So where the man was allowin' us maybe five or six dollars to the plow, he quit. After that, most of the black people moved to the city. They had no choice. When the man with the tractor come in, the black people had to go to the city in order to get a job in order to survive. Very few of 'em had land of their own."

The old black man left the country for awhile himself, traveling to Indiana, New York, and Pennsylvania to work in the steel mills and the coal mines. But unlike many black men who left the land, he came back to it. He bought seven acres and built a house only two miles from where he was born. That accomplishment makes him proud. There's only one thing that bothers him. "Back then," he says, "we had a freedom to hunt. People was more neighborly about lettin' you on their land. Today it ain't so easy to find a good place to hunt."

It's the great irony in the old black man's life.

But not everyone is convinced access to land is a major problem. Hear a landowner ask the question: "Do you know anybody who really likes to hunt, I'm talking about a regular fellow who's not a game hog, not a drunk, but a good, decent fellow, who doesn't have a place to hunt?" Hear the landowner answer, "I don't know anybody and I've been around a good while." One paper company in the South leases 60% of its massive holdings to some 250 hunting clubs for $1.50 to $2.00 an acre. The company keeps the remaining 40% wide open. Anybody can walk in and get a permit. "The damn trouble with the hunting public is that most of them are unwilling to go to any trouble. They want a place within 10 miles of the house, and they will come to you wanting a permit for some place close but that nobody else can get to. There ain't no damn such thing. There are thousands of acres in this state on corporate holdings and public hunting areas that if a guy would take the trouble to get a map and find out where to go and be willing to pick a place that's farther than a quarter of a mile from the road, he could have a place to hunt. But a lot of 'em are too damn lazy to do it. The hunting public wants the world to be like it was in 1880, when we loaded our guns and walked out the back door and started hunting at the fence. It is no longer that way. If you aren't willin' to drive 70-80 miles, sell your shotgun."

Goodloe Sutton tries to understand all sides of the land access issue. That's his job. He is publisher and editor of the *Linden Democrat Reporter* weekly newspaper. He has a tremendous knack for sensing the town's mood about a subject and then putting that mood into words on the editorial page. Sutton feels the frustration of the local guy who's hunted a certain piece of property all of his life only to go out and find it posted one day. He also recognizes the landowner's desire to run a lodge or lease land for the money. He emphasizes that retail stores, gas stations and other businesses benefit from the arrival of an out of county hunter. But what Sutton doesn't condone, in fact they downright infuriate him, are the outlaw poachers from both in and out of state.

There are an increasing number of hunter slobs who hunt at night with flashlights, who shoot from the roads, who come in by boat, who slaughter herds, who damage property, who sell deer meat, and who frequently cause a shooting death or injury in the woods. Poaching is a deepening problem and will continue to be so as hunting access dwindles and deer and turkey populations increase. But Sutton doesn't take to those who use their lack of access to land as an excuse for poaching. After a series of violent incidents, and the week after hunters from another county shot up a Linden restaurant and lounge and wounded the owner, Sutton wrote: "We see one sure way to put an end to this violent

carnage being perpetrated by people with absolutely no ties here
and less concern for the rest of us. We can simply forbid everybody from
other states and other counties to come into Marengo County to hunt.
Crazy? Not so crazy when compared with the rationale for the recent
killings and shootings. People here have been slow to anger. We sense
that anger rising."

Sutton has also been very outspoken about his local court's handling of
poaching and other violation cases. He became personally involved several years ago. "My aunt and I were cutting through these bushes getting
closer to a turkey," he says with southern gentlemanly charm. "Suddenly
we heard this Bam-Bam-Bam. Leaves started falling all over us. I eased
forward a little bit and saw this guy bending over the turkey. I told him to
stand right there. If he'd a raised his gun I would have killed him. But he

broke and ran." Sutton had the man arrested, but the court cleared him on a "tiny, tiny technicality," which Sutton suspects may or may not have had a great deal to do with certain friendships involving certain participants in the case from the legal profession. Sutton fought back with several biting editorials denouncing the court's leniency. He says the right people apparently received his message. The court has since gotten tougher on violators.

But poaching is by no means easy to control. It never has been. Not only is the violator tough to locate, but he can be hell to take in. Some years ago a game warden encountered a man poaching for turkey, which in some remote areas is about the worst crime in the world, even worse than shooting a man's dog. The game warden hollered at the intruder to stop but the fellow took off. The game warden pulled out his .45 automatic and shot the man in the leg. The man fell, got up, and started running. The game warden shot him again, in the shoulder this time, and sent him head over heels. But the poacher got to his feet, ran to the river, and swam across. Two months later, the game warden caught the same man poaching the same area.

On the front porch of a small house on a country road, 76-year-old Melvin Dukes packs his gear for a three-day hunting outing. Hunting game is how Dukes has lived much of his life the past 10 years, which is healthier than hunting men, which was Dukes' job as one of those troubleshooting game wardens for the state from 1956 until he retired in 1974. Dukes is a character and he knows it. His thick, scraggily, gray beard drapes down to the zipper of an aqua parker, and considering he stands only an inch or two above five feet the hairy mass does not have far to flow until it brushes the tops of his white rubber boots. He tucks the bill of a green Levi Garrett hat over his eyes. So here is a man with the face of a hat and a beard, except when the story is good. When the story is good his eyes flicker and shine at you. When it's good, Melvin Dukes' rough voice, the kind of voice that has his listeners swallowing for him, will spit out words faster than a Gatling gun.

Dukes didn't become a game warden until the age of 44. (It was a decision he regretted only once—when alligator jumped from 50 cents to six dollars a foot. "I was tempted to quit the state and go gator huntin'," he says.) A young Dukes butchered meat for several years. He managed a yacht for a rich yankee for three years. He served four years, one month, 26 days, and two and a half hours in the army, and during 31 months overseas crossed North Africa, Sicily, and Italy. "I didn't see it, but I was right there within a few miles when they hung ole Mussolini upside down." He returned to the butchering business after his stint and six years later bought his own store. He made a profit, sold it, and became a game warden, a position suited to his heart's desire to be outdoors and closer to game and guns. "When my eyes were good I was as good as there were anywhere with a gun," he grins. "They mighta been better people with a rifle, but I never did shoot against any of 'em." Dukes knew his position would also bring him closer to outlaws, but he considered enforcement a necessary task for someone, so why not him, a man born in the country, raised hunting, and disciplined in life-and-death confrontations by his military tenure.

"When you're workin' with hunters you're workin' with somebody that has a gun and they will shoot you," Dukes says. He pulls up the bill of his cap and reveals a scar on the upper right of his forehead. He tugs the cap back down. "That was a night hunter did that."

Dukes and his partner had pulled in behind three night hunters who had loaded a spike buck in the back of their car. Dukes saw the man sitting on the passenger side draw his shotgun. "He would have got us if I hadn't seen the gun come out," Dukes says. "I hollered 'look out he's gonna shoot us' and he let two loads of it go." The car full of poachers moved out, with Dukes and his partner, who was driving, in pursuit. A run and gun battle ensued. "Everytime they'd make a left hand turn they'd shoot at us," Dukes says. "Oh I shot their car, I think I shot 17 holes in it, but I didn't ever put 'em in the right place." After a 12 mile chase, the outlaws' vehicle hit a mud hole and grounded out. "But you know two of them guys jumped out of that car and I know they was doin' 40-50 miles an hour," says Dukes, who received his wound sometime during the melee. "We went back and found where they'd hit the ground." Dukes and his partner captured all three before daylight. Dukes had had a run-in with the man

doing the shooting two years earlier. "He'd shot a deer and I eased up on him and put the light on him," Dukes says. "He spun around but I was close enough to grab the gun and keep him from shootin'. Oh Dukes, he says, killin' deer is one thing but I wouldn't shoot nobody. My God he was the one pullin' the damn trigger two years later."

Dukes tells another story he wasn't involved in, of another warden checking on hunters crossing the state line by way of the river and poaching on a private club's land. The warden combed the area and found a boat pulled up to shore with a 218B rifle in it. He left the boat and the gun, went back to his car and radioed the tower to call his wife and tell her he didn't know what time he'd be in. When he returned to the boat two men were in it preparing to leave. Dressed in uniform with a .357 on his belt, the warden approached the men and told them to come out of the boat. They didn't oblige. When the warden stepped on the end of the boat one of the men reached for a gun. The warden began wrestling with the man and the gun but the warden fell overboard. "When that warden come up, he come up shootin'," Dukes says. The warden shot one man through the arm, but was shot in the hand himself. The men sped away, but were later apprehended in their state. "It cost 'em some money, but that's all," Dukes says. "I told our prosecutor if I ever get between those son-of-a-bitches and the state line by God there won't be no damn trial."

Dukes would have handled the matter differently had he encountered the boat with the rifle in it. "If I'd seen the rifle, I'd said well their comin' back and I'd a took that rifle out. I'd had my shotgun and I'd been standin' behind a tree. I'd a never got out without the shotgun if I was by myself. When they'd a come back there they'd a never got back in that boat. I'd a stepped out and had my gun and asked those fellas to lay their guns down. I don't know why he (the warden) went back to the car. My wife don't even know when I'm coming back."

The light penalty the court gave the criminals didn't surprise Dukes, who says judges today are doing a better job of backing up game wardens than they did in his time. "You can get a bad judge," he says. "We had one here. He did pretty good for awhile and then he decided to get into politics. He started turnin' 'em loose so he wouldn't lose their vote. I caught a fella with 32 squirrels, eight's the limit, and that son-of-a-bitch judge turned him loose. I said, 'But judge he had 32,' and the judge said, 'Well, they were kind of skinny weren't they.' "

Dukes contributed to the judge's removal from office. "There aren't many mailboxes I don't know in this county," he says. "I didn't get out and make any stump speeches, but we whipped his ass. We whipped him with a woman who made a damn good judge."

In a small town at a chamber of commerce luncheon, a short, compact elderly man with the state pounds the podium. He challenges a full house that if somebody told them a half-billion dollar business was in trouble, they would put on their marching boots and do something about it. He pulls out slides and shows the audience how his business, the conservation program, touches the hotel man, the insurance man, the hardware man, the grocery man, and every kind of man sitting before his eyes. "The business community has to recognize the importance of this as a business," he emphasizes. "And the conservation business is sick, and it's going to get sicker if it don't get some strong arm support."

The man speaks with 25 years of experience. His name is Charles Kelly. The picture he paints to this audience is a bleak one. But if it's shaky now, consider 50 years ago in the state when deer and turkey numbers combined possibly reached 20,000. That figure has increased to 1.2 million deer and 400,000 turkey.

What happened?

Men like Charles Kelly settled on the philosophy: You won't have much wildlife unless you commit an overt act to have it.

"We said to the landowner, you raise it, you can kill it, legitimately," Charles Kelly says. "Suddenly there was a greater desire on the part of the landowner to see that deer eat a few more soybeans. When the deer season opened he and his friends could go out and kill a buck deer every damn day of the season."

Other states chastised Kelly's program. They called it too liberal. They said it was crazy. They said a 62-day buck season with a deer every damn day would force the state out of the deer business. They were wrong; 1.2 million deer wrong. "There's been a 180 degree shift in the attitude of the public," Kelly says. "I can remember if you were to go to north Alabama and release six deer in the morning, they'd have five packs of dogs on the ground that afternoon. You go to north Alabama now and release six deer and somebody puts a pack of dogs on them, that somebody better be prepared to get out of the country."

Other developments occurred through the years as well. As private land-owners began posting keep out signs, Kelly's team began scratching for public game management areas for those kept out to hunt in. When landowners began hollering poacher, Kelly's troubleshooters went to work. A successful program? Yes. But to Kelly it's far from where it should be. His between-the-lines message to the chamber is this: The South needs more money to hire enough good men like Melvin Dukes to apprehend a growing number of poachers; more money to continue innovating game programs with landowners such as the Stimpsons; more money to maintain quality hunting land available to the public.

The gathering gets the message. There goes the hat.

THE EQUIPMENT

It is just about time for dinner and the sun cuts a lukewarm swath through the dry, wispy January air. In the South, dinner is the meal that falls somewhere in between breakfast and supper. But the boys who are hovering around The Bucket don't seem overly anxious to be getting home.

The Bucket is a combination filling station, convenience store, and hunting supplies headquarters right in the middle of what could be any small Southern town, just up from the Brighter Day Restaurant and Community House and just across the street from Jane's Cash Store.

. In front of Jane's, maybe five old black men sit on rusted metal gliders and share what warmth there is, along with a couple or three of the best stories they've heard lately. All the while, they keep a steady but impassive eye on the hunters who orbit The Bucket.

Hunters are beginning to stop by after early morning forays into deer-dappled woods. Three fellows are hunched over the sides of the bed of a Chevy pick up. They are smoking cigarettes without the use of hands, looking at an eight point buck.

The Bucket parking lot is where, if you are a hunter, you will most likely stop and show your kill on Saturday. It's the unofficial but widely-recognized seat of government for game stalkers in the area.

Inside The Bucket, there are two separate departments. Food is sold in one: Cheese crackers, soft drinks, candy bars, kosher dills in a big glass jar, Skol (which is often as important as food), beer, and the like. On Saturday, there is a steady stream of patrons who saunter in to the shadowy old store with grins on their faces and mosey over to the drink box or pick up a pack of peanuts at the counter. They all have something to say to the man in charge of the store. His name is Luther. While the

one department specializes in the sale of food, the other is filled with everything a man could use to go out and kill his own. This other department is the one Luther prefers.

Luther was born and raised here, (in fact, he was born in the back of Jane's Cash Store) and is pretty small for a man who kills bear for sport, which he does in Canada every now and then. Around the county, he sticks mainly to turkey and deer. Good thing. Last time anybody saw a bear around these parts, the South was an independent republic. Luther even goes so far as to wear a bear claw necklace, and he keeps a picture of himself and a buddy on The Bucket bulletin board. They are

standing self-consciously beside two recently killed bears. Of course,
they are the only bear hunters on this board in this small town. The balance of the space is reserved for turkey and deer.

The deer hunting is especially good here, and every man who suc-
ceeds in killing something to be proud of takes it around to Luther so
Luther can take his picture with one of those cameras that spits the picture
right out.

This practice can't be bad for business. In fact, it must be pretty darn
good. Luther says he sold over 600 rifles, shotguns, and pistols the previous year. That's not bad retailing for a town whose entire downtown
district might consist of only one or two stores.

"Hey, Luther," a young man yells across the store. "Come out here and
take a look at this new dog I got." Luther disappears for a few minutes, then returns with the young man right behind him. "That hound's
'bout as ugly's I've seen 'round here," Luther says.

The young man winks and clucks at Luther as he's grabbing a pint of chocolate milk from the cooler. "Yeah, but he's a good dog from what I hear."

Luther, though not an old man by any means, prides himself on being the acknowledged learned sage of hunting around the town. It shows in the way he greets his customers, and in the way he answers their questions. "The right basic hunting equipment: good boots, warm clothes, and a nice gun are what you need," says Luther.

The hunters around town gravitate to Luther at The Bucket, almost as if they needed to square themselves with Luther before a day of hunting is really complete. They're like Little Leaguers running up to the coach to ask if the homerun they just slammed was a good hit. Stroking. That's what makes The Bucket The Bucket.

The Rod 'n Gun Sports Center and shops with similar names and emphasis are larger, more sophisticated versions of The Bucket. They are usually found in the larger towns across the South. You can't buy a snack here, or a pouch of Red Man, but there is more than triple the equipment.

Jim, who works most Saturdays, is very cordial, and will even take the time to explain the ins and outs of bream fishing to an obvious novice just off the plane from New Jersey, while several serious deer hunters and quail men wait on him to hand over some shells.

But The Rod 'n Gun doesn't care how good you are, or what you've killed, they just want to help you decide on some type of equipment to buy. Unlike The Bucket, this place does not operate for a handful of locals, but for the masses.

Let's say a perfect stranger wanted to take up hunting. You can bet Jim would be more than happy to help the stranger get started. Get him on the path to a lifetime of hunting adventure. "How much would all this cost?" he might wonder. Jim would be glad to provide the answer.

For instance, in most places, you're going to hunt, but you're going to need a license. That'll be $10. You'll need warm clothing, and if you opt for one of those camouflaged one-piece jump suits, you'll pay about $52. Of course, you'll want a hat. Another $10. Waterproof boots will set you back about $50, but if you want leather, it's about $100. Gloves go for

about $20. A good knife, $30. A new shotgun can cost between $200 and $10,000. This is a decision every hunter must make for himself. After you get the gun, you might consider buying a pistol, for killing snakes and finishing off game. $130 on the average. You'll definitely need shells. Two boxes, let's say $25. And after you buy all that stuff, you're going to need a place to do your hunting. That can be the tough part. You could buy a permit to hunt on land owned by some of the large paper companies, $10 or so. Or you might want to be assured of good hunting lands with a minimum of people on it so you could join a hunting club, if they'll have you. Say $250 to $500 per year.

And we haven't even mentioned the cost of a dog, if you want one of those, too.

By the time you kill your first buck, or bird, and it might be a while before you do, you're going to have spent at least $1,000 for it, probably much, much more. And if you get a buck, you'll probably want to have it mounted. $175 to $200.

Of course, there are those who get really carried away when it comes to hunting equipment. According to hunting guide and writer Wayne Fears, the pursuit of new and exclusive—and expensive—equipment is very good for the avid hunter. It gives him something to do in the summer besides sitting around wishing it were hunting season.

Once upon a time, the Southern hunter relied upon a good gun, a good dog, a sturdy pair of boots and his wits. Today, if you believe what you read in the mail-order catalogues, you know that these few things won't even begin to cover it. A great American once said, "Take care of your equipment, and your equipment will take care of you." If today's hunters tried to take care of all the equipment available to them, they would never have time to go hunting. Some of the gear they are offering in catalogues and magazines is enough to make the boys at The Bucket fall out of their pick-ups.

For some reason, 4-wheel drive vehicles have come into vogue. Hunters can't seem to stay away from them, and neither, it should be noted, can their wives. Where once the wood-paneled station wagon stood as the ultimate status symbol of upwardly mobile mothers, there now stands the 4-wheel drive.

Vehicles aside, there is a wealth of hunting accessories to be had for a price. There are bird bags and quail vests and chaps that slip over a

hunter's pants to keep him from being snake bit. There are duck decoys and anchors and duck calls of all description. There are camouflaged stools and chairs, camouflaged flotation cushions and camouflaged thermos bottles. There are insulated camouflaged waders and compasses that you pin on yourself. Camouflaged gun cleaning kits, pistol and rifle cases and gun racks.

There are binoculars and shooting glasses. Hunter's seats, scents and lures, and portable deer stands. There are recoil pads, hearing protectors, and leather bags to carry shotgun shell boxes. There are tents, camp stoves, camp ovens, and griddles. Hide-Away saws, first-aid kits, rescue blankets, and submersible flashlights.

All-weather lanterns, waterproof duffle bags, and utility boxes. There are camouflaged day packs, fanny packs, and knap sacks. Sleeping bags good to −10 degrees, fold-up cots, and fishnet underwear to keep you dry in important places.

For dogs there are dog beds, cedar filled. Electric training prods and choke collars. There are leather dog boots and rubber dog boots. There is toothpaste for dogs. And there are septic tanks for dogs. There are reversible camouflaged coats to keep dogs warm and there are dog life preservers to keep them floating if they forget how to swim.

There is even gear for hunters to use when they aren't hunting. For instance, dog head belt buckles, highball glasses with ducks etched on the sides. Canine sportswear, canine coffee mugs, and canines molded out of sterling silver that you wear around your neck.

There are suspenders that say, "I'd Rather Be Hunting." There are T-shirts that sport the phrase, "We Interrupt This Marriage To Bring You Hunting Season."

There are Christmas ornaments in the shape of game and dogs, there are ties with dog prints on them and hats with dogs' faces on them. There are camouflaged place mats and napkins, mallard-shaped night-lights and bath towels with mallards printed on them.

There are stacking tables, each with a different hunting scene painted on its vinyl top and there are personalized plaques you can have custom made to pay tribute to your dog. There are retrievers on thermometers and pointers on clocks.

"It's amazing," says Fears. "We get these guys who come in here with so much gear, they can't even make it into their bedrooms."

In addition to his writing and hunting trips, Fears owns several hunting lodges in some of the South's most densely-wooded, sparsely populated areas. These lodges of Fears' cater to hunters from all over the United States, and one of Fears' favorite stories is about one of those hunters a few years back. A man from New York City.

He arrived at the old hunting lodge wearing a purple polyester leisure suit. Wayne introduced him to the other hunters like a mother who has been called into a meeting of the varsity football squad to introduce her bespectacled young son, the poet, as a new member of the team.

He was the thorough embodiment of the urban north. They were Southern as grits and gravy biscuits.

These hunters had probably never even met a man wearing a leisure suit. They just didn't know what to make of him. Like a bunch of puppies, making the acquaintance of a porcupine. They were the type of men who neither understand nor appreciate shopping malls, hotel discos, or people who say they "feel good about themselves." They were out-doorsmen. Serious hunters. And they were here at Wayne's place looking for trophy bucks to take home and put on their walls next to the ones already there.

So, this descendant of a Union soldier—just to break the ice—announces that he had never before in his life shot a rifle. Never even held one. The group of hunters, each one a veteran of grueling and successful hunts all over the world, took to the northerner's news with subdued surprise, like a Sunday morning preacher might if handed a note informing him that his fly was open.

But this New York fellow was a friendly sort. Real outgoing and easy to like. He told the group over dinner that while he had never had anything to do with hunting, he did happen to have a lot of money, and with that money he just up and decided to buy himself a ticket South to see what hunting was all about. To see if it was all that the magazines make it out to be. To try something new. Give hunting a shot, so to speak.

The other hunters began to warm up to this purple pistol from the big city, even though they fully expected him to head back to the safety of New York as soon as he realized how tough it is to be successful hunting. The thought of this novice out there by himself in a stand in the woods made them grin into their coffee cups.

Next morning, while the experienced hunters were out in their stands waiting on the trophy bucks, Wayne took this rank beginner, still dressed in his purple leisure suit, to the firing range and gave him a rifle. Fears showed him how to load and unload, told him what to do and what not to do. Fears then led him up to the firing line and told him to let loose with five or six shots just to get the feel of things. The northerner did. Got a bull's-eye every time.

"The guy was a natural shot," Fears said later. "I just couldn't believe it."

After lunch that same day, everyone began making preparations to go out again after the trophy bucks. None had been killed that morning.

The hunters made their ways downstairs to meet Fears. They wore camouflage and had painted their faces. All gear was shipshape and ready to be of use on the hunt. They were prepared.

Their northern companion bounced down the stairs a few minutes later. He had on the purple leisure suit. On his feet, a smart pair of loafers. As they picked their jaws up off the floor, the northerner told his comrades he wouldn't dream of wearing all that stuff. The other hunters began giving old purple puss a hard time about his indifference to hunting decorum. But the New Yorker just grinned in the face of all their criticism and set about at a leisurely pace in his leisurely suit toward the door.

Fears took the other hunters to their respective blinds first and wished them all well. Then he proceeded to the last blind with his purple neophyte in tow. Fears gave the man a crash course in how to bag a buck, and with a shake of his head, left him to his own devices.

"I just told him, 'Stay here and don't try and wander off,'" Fears said. "I knew he would see some deer, but I didn't expect too much action out of him." He was a joke. "Damn fool Yankee," the other hunters said. "If I hadn't seen him with my own two eyes, I wouldn't have thought somebody like that could exist, except on TV."

That night, Fears went around picking up all the hunters, saving his collection of the purple New Yorker for last. The other hunters, though none had bagged a trophy buck, started in right away laughing and carrying on about their cohort from New York. Laughing about how he was probably shivering in his loafers by now. And about how he was probably frightened to death at being left out in the middle of the woods at night with nary a subway in sight.

When Fears and the rest of the boys drove up to where the New Yorker was standing, they didn't even give him a chance to speak. They just started in on him right away about how his purple leisure suit must have been a sight for all those deer that passed by. That maybe the purple suit had scared the deer away from the entire county, and so forth.

The man from the north took the ribbing calmly, very quietly. Then, like the Cheshire Cat, a grin began to spread across his face. And he very matter-of-factly mentioned that he had a "big deer" over there across the field, and would they be so kind as to help him get it to the truck.

Fears and the rest of the men looked at one another suspiciously, and then went over to check on this claim. There, they found a beautiful 10-point buck. The New Yorker had drilled it with one shot.

The hunting party got kind of quiet after that.

After dinner, the New Yorker, still wearing his purple leisure suit, said goodnight and went to bed. The other hunters said to each other that it was just beginner's luck. Pure luck. Somebody called him the purple phantom. And then they all started calling him the purple phantom.

"No way this purple phantom's gonna hit anything else," they said. "No-body's that damn lucky."

At dawn the next day, everyone was up getting ready for another day in the stands. The other hunters were certain that this would be the day they would bag the trophy buck. Again, they decked themselves out in the camouflage. Again, they painted their faces. And again, the purple phantom wore his purple leisure suit and loafers.

The other hunters just looked at each other.

Fears went to pick them all up again around 11 a.m. They had had a little success, but only a little. There were two killed between all of them—all except the purple phantom. They saved the trip to his stand for last.

When they got to the spot where Fears had left the phantom, it was only natural that more than one of them had to take a second look. Bagged another one. An 8 point.

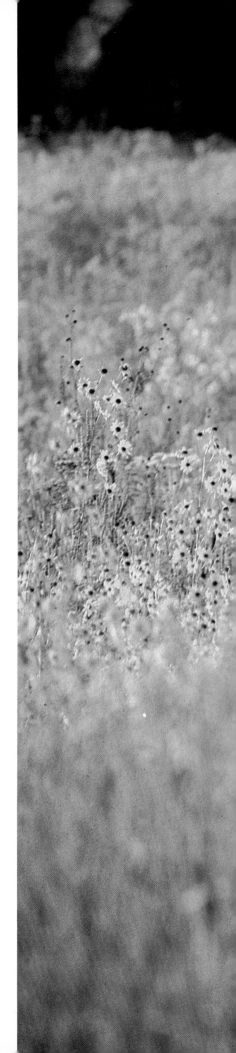

Well, the purple phantom became a pretty popular fellow after that. The other hunters couldn't figure it out. All they knew was that this New Yorker, this purple phantom, who had never even seen a deer outside of a zoo and who had never even held a rifle until yesterday, was sitting here with a 10 point and an 8 point to his credit. This guy was not a hunter, he was a magician. He couldn't be a hunter. He wasn't dressed for it.

The purple phantom announced to the group that he would take his leave of the hunting party and head back to New York. This was on the morning of the third day, an hour or so after he had killed his third deer. A buck. Seven point.

The phantom stood up at lunch and told his chagrined companions that he would be giving up hunting for good. That he didn't think he would ever feel compelled to try it again, because, oh, how could he put this, there just wasn't enough challenge to it.

He left soon after that and was swallowed up by the jungle he knew best. Fears nor any of the rest of the hunters ever heard from the purple phantom again.

"He became a legend around here," Fears says. "The legend of the purple phantom."

And just think what he could have done with a decent pair of boots, some camouflage, a custom rifle, some face paint, and a cap of his own.

Perhaps in Tallapoosa County, some distance away from Wayne Fears' hunting lodges, the purple phantom could have found a more challenging adventure in hunting. Perhaps, if he had come here, he would have declared himself a lifelong follower of sports afield. But it didn't happen like that, so Tallapoosa County will remain, for now, free of purple leisure suits, and filled with hunters. None of whom are more well known than those hunters lucky enough to be hooked up with The Dixie Hunting Club.

On a misty December day, during the second to the last deer drive of the season, there are, say, 25 pick ups in the dirt parking lot that adjoins the old colored school. Twenty-three are either Chevy, Ford, or GMC. Another, a Toyota, has been slyly painted over at the tailgate so the white "Toyota" name does not stand out. It is a curious sight, leading a visitor to believe that in this county of highly-patriotic textile workers, the buying of a Japanese import is barely tolerated at best, and then only if the buyer doesn't appear proud of it.

After all, textile workers, who make up probably 80 percent of the Dixie Hunting Club's membership, can relate to the threat of foreign imports. They make no bones about it.

And truthfully, alongside all the other American pick ups in the lot, the two from Japan almost seem embarrassed.

The Dixie Hunting Club is made up of 100 or so God-fearing individuals who—you guessed it—love to hunt. A man or woman lucky enough to be a member of the club—which holds the lease on 11,000 acres of prime hunting land, including shoreline, pine plantations, and hardwood stands—is sure to be expert in the ways of hunting, as well as very expert at abiding the club rules. There are plenty.

For instance, there's no hunting on Sunday. That's the Lord's day. No unruly behavior of any kind allowed under any circumstances. Guns aren't allowed in the clubhouse; everyone parks them along the blistered, once-white front of the school house before they go in.

There's no shooting over the legal limit, which only makes sense, and whiskey isn't allowed anywhere near the place. Anyone in the club caught smoking marijuana would likely be shot. Plus, everybody but everybody who hunts for deer must wear a certain amount of hunter's orange, or else they just can't go. No exceptions.

The deer drive is set to begin early on Saturday morning. There are three planned for the day, and around 6:30 the yawning hunters, around 60 of them, begin filing into the old colored schoolhouse in anticipation of the event. Of course, at that time of day, the most important piece of equipment on any hunt is the coffee pot, and around that is where most of the hunters are gathered. There, and around two old space heaters set up to ward off the damp chill in the air. Several of the club officers are making arrangement for the assigning of deer stands and are taking up dues.

To some hunters, how you look is half of it. Not so where members of the Dixie Hunting Club are concerned. Looks are not everything to this bunch of woodsmen and women. For instance, there are teenaged members who show up in blue jeans and camouflaged shirts. They wear the same thing to school around here. There are the older hunters who come dressed in the old red hunting coats from back in the days before they discovered it was safer to wear orange in the woods to protect against being shot. Back then, they said red was the safest color. They were wrong. A few, very few, are suited up in the one piece Gortex jump suits with the new bark design, as opposed to the leaf design. Some say the bark is better for hunters who like to take their shots while leaning up against a tree. These suits are fairly expensive and most members of the club just dress in the most comfortable hunting clothes they happen to own and leave it at that. One or two, like the retired preacher here today, throw caution to the wind and show up in just plain clothes.

The preacher's suit is composed of a plaid coat and an unmatching pair of plaid pants. He's wearing street shoes. But at least he's wearing a hunter's orange vest over all this, so he appears somewhat legitimate. That is, if you can keep from looking at his shoes, and how they are a good seven inches away from the bottom of his trousers. The preacher is joking and joining in with the rest of the members. He's probably been wearing that plaid on plaid suit for years.

No. Sporty dress is not required for members of the Dixie Hunting Club. You just wear what comes natural, or you wear something synthetic, and on top of it all you wear orange.

Of course, if you were looking for something that members of the club take very seriously, that would have to be their guns. In the mornings and between each hunt, they are leaned with care up against the wall of the clubhouse, just near the door. These guns are in excellent condition. Each looking as if it were spit shined the night before. Not a speck of rust anywhere. Their grains show up beautifully against the old wall. Lined up like they are, they look like a legion of ebony soldiers prepared to march into war.

It can never be said of the Dixie Hunting Club that they skimp on the maintenance of their guns. They may be wearing pants that were bought before Elvis was king. They may be driving mud-caked old Fords with dented hoods and faded political stickers on the fenders, but by God their shotguns could pass Patton's inspection. There's something between a man and his gun that makes it mandatory for this to happen, if the man expects to hold his head up in a crowd of his peers. Of course, there are several lady members, too. And their guns are just as clean as the rest of them.

There is a very set way that the hunters are assigned stands. It's done with numbers. All the numbers are kept in a box and drawn by the huntmaster, or the secretary, or someone else with an honest face and reputation. There is no favoritism involved in who gets what stand. If there was, the Dixie Hunting Club would probably have gone belly up years ago.

After each hunt , before the deer are hoisted up in the air and weighed, the dead deer's jaw is removed with a set of instruments that would make even the most sadistic dentist weak in the knees and catch his breath. It's a big triangular piece of steel that is inserted into the deer's mouth by one person, while another cuts, pulls and tears the jaw loose by whatever means possible. While this is going on, members of the club are standing around watching, eating snacks. The jaw is later sent to the State Department of Conservation and Natural Resources so it can determine just how old the deer was before it met up with a sure-shotted member of the Dixie Hunting Club.

Certain members of the club are referred to as "dog men." Not because they look or smell like dogs, but because they own one or more of them. These "dog men" keep their dogs in dog boxes placed on the backs of their pick ups. These particular dog boxes have not been mail ordered from some equipment magazine. They are handmade. Fashioned out of plywood, with little holes in them so the dogs can breathe. Mostly, the dog lays down or crouches there because there's no room to stand up. Between hunts, there comes through the crowd the mournful whines of the dogs, sometimes high, sometimes low-pitched. It's the dogs' way of letting everyone know they are ready to get after the deer.

Even though keeping a dog closed in a little box might seem a bit heavy-handed, every authority on the subject will agree that it is far better to use the dog box than to let the dog just hang on for dear life once the truck gets going.

Lucy Landers is one of the members of the club, in fact, she's a charter member and an officer. Because of Lucy, hunting in this county—unlike many—is very much a sport for both sexes. There are usually four to seven women who regularly hunt with the club. It's something you wouldn't expect way down South in the rural counties.

Aside from her duties as treasurer, though, and despite the fact that she is probably one of the best hunters in the bunch, Lucy will not hesitate to tell you—a la Julia Child—the best way to cook a deer after you've gone out and laid one to rest. According to Lucy, all you do to deer meat if you want it to turn out good is to cook it just like you would any other meat of a similar cut. You don't have to marinate it or baste it with some kind of special sauce. A lot of people think that venison must be of an unusual nature, wild, or slightly dirtier than steer meat, pig meat, or chicken meat.

"Oh no," Lucy Landers says. "I just treat a cut of venison like I would the same cut of beef." And Lucy Landers should know about these things. She's been killing, cooking, and eating deer meat for some time now. And although "deerburgers" are not exactly a household staple in this country, according to Lucy ground deer meat is just as tasty as ground beef.

And even though there are many people like Lucy Landers who swear by the delicious nature of venison, many others would just as soon spend their time and money hunting deer in order to gain the deer itself, not just the meat on its bones.

These are the trophy collectors. The people who pay to have their kill removed from its skin, stuffed with wood shavings, painted, and in many other ways prepared as an ornament to be hung on a wall or placed on a shelf.

The Hunt

On a lazy Sunday afternoon in the country, after churches have been let out for the day, clans of black tenant farming families sit in ancient chairs on their front porches and watch the day's allotment of cars amble down their rural roads in the late October heat.

It's the tail end of dove season, and the locals know what to expect: Droves of cars from the city. Cars carrying hopeful hunters, many with their sons in tow.

The hunters have been making this same seasonal pilgrimage to nearby dove fields for as long as any porch front observer can remember.

Communication between these two groups consists of an occasional wave and a mutual understanding of what each side is doing. Nothing more.

It's not too unusual for a motorist driving through this fertile farming country to have his car sprayed with rifle shot during the season. Most take "peppering" as a good sign. It means the dove are flying.

But just down the road a ways, at the Hale Plantation, there is reason to believe they won't be flying too much today. A nearby farmer has just harvested 1,000 acres of corn, leaving plenty of fat kernels behind. Why should the dove go anywhere else?

Sunday dove shoots are a tradition at the Hale Plantation, and today is no different. Dr. Everett Hale is not too downcast over the prospect of too few doves, for he isn't hosting this dove shoot solely for the pleasure of gunning down birds. He looks upon these shoots as the essence of socializing.

"What I like most about a dove shoot is being outdoors during this time of year with my friends," says Hale, a big man with thick white hair complemented by longish sideburns that taper off in a point.

Hale and his brother Bradley inherited the 2,000-acre former cotton plantation from his father. Now, most of it is leased out to corn, wheat and soybean farmers, who are carefully instructed by Hale to leave strips of underbrush around the edges of the fields to provide cover for quail.

Hale keeps several fields planted in brown top millet and milo and it's around the former his dove shoot is to take place. The shoot is to begin at 2 p.m., but his camouflaged guests and their sons start showing up around 12:30, kind of sheepish for being so early. Many refer to Hale as "Squire."

These premature guests take a seat on the wide screened front porch that overlooks the fishing pond and the rolling fields of golden rod, black-eyed Susans and white tops.

Hale stands inside before the over-sized, unlit fireplace that's none-the-less loaded with logs on this 90-degree day, and wolfs down a barbecue sandwich. Flanking the fireplace on either side are two trophy bucks felled by Hale's son-in-law, Robert, but Hale takes no part in deer hunting.

"There's a big difference in shooting something flying through the air above your head and sitting in a tree shooting down at something the size of a cow," Hale says.

"There's no comparison to me."

The man Hale calls "Black Robert" (to distinguish him from Hale's white son-in-law) is outside the modest main house making an attempt to round up a litter of wildish kittens.

"Anybody out there want to take home a cat?" Hale calls out to his guests. Grunts and moans answer his query. "Robert's had a hell of a time rounding them up, especially since Katie got here." More grunts and moans.

Hale's black lab, Katie, is a middle-aged retriever with a good disposition, a soft mouth and one eye usually turned on Hale.

Around 2:00, after the previous day's ball game has been critiqued and digested, the hunters, about 40 of them, load up in their pick-ups and cars and caravan off to the dove field.

Each posts himself, with directions from Hale, in separate stands around two adjoining fields, each about the size of a football gridiron. Almost immediately, shots ring out over the freshly cut millet and three or four birds sputter and flutter toward Earth, hitting the ground with tiny thumps.

Every so often, shot rains down from the sky over where Hale is situated.

The air on this warm Indian summer day is still and humid. The hunters keep making trips back to their cars or dipping into their camouflaged coolers for cold beer and soft drinks.

During a lull in the doves' flight, one of the hunters joins another to pass the time, wiping his face with a bloody handkerchief.

"Other day we were on a shoot down around Greene County," he says with squenched eyes scanning the sky. "This fellow from out of town got bored and shot a barn swallow. Damn song bird. There weren't any doves flying and he just got tired of sitting there. Game warden came along and slapped him with a hundred dollar fine."

"Did he pay it?" the other hunter asked, chuckling.

"No, we did. He was one of our clients."

Hale isn't doing much shooting, but occasionally when he spots an easy mark, he swings his 20-gauge to the sky and lets loose two shots—bam!bam!—in quick fashion. The gun fits into the crook of his shoulder as if it were a third arm, as if the three-foot long piece of iron and wood were a natural extension of Hale's large frame.

Several hours into the hunt, Hale and Katie load up in Hale's ancient Ford pick-up and ramble around the field checking on his guests.

"How you doing, Tom?"

"Oh, I don't know. Can't hit 'em like I used to."

"How many'd you get?"

"Half dozen maybe."

Hale rounds a bend and comes upon one of his friends standing there in his blind laughing.

"What's so funny, Hilliard?"

"That young fellow over there," he answers, pointing to a teenaged boy nearby.

"He cusses a blue streak between every shot. I don't know what the matter could be, because he's killing some. I guess that's just his style."

Around 5, the hunters begin to straggle up to Hale's truck in pairs, most carrying their game in pouches hooked around their waists.

"Great shoot, Squire," they say. "Sure had a good time, Everett."

"Now y'all don't run off," Hale tells each one. "There's sandwiches up at the house and maybe a little red eye whiskey, too."

Hale points out a little red house off in the distance as he drives back to the main house. That's where Minnie lives.

"Minnie's lived here all her life," Hale says. "We don't charge her rent, since her husband's dead and she's on her own now. But she pays us back by cleaning birds." Hale drives a little closer to the house for a better look. "She's not usually at home on Sundays. Stays in church most of the day or visiting around. It's a pretty good arrangement for me. I don't have to take all these birds back home for my wife to clean."

Back at the house, some of the guests are kicking around in the dirt of the driveway, saying their goodbyes and making the usual excuses as to why they didn't kill anymore than they did.

"Sun was right in my eyes."

"New gun."

"Every time they got close, I was changing dern shells."

Others are milling around inside eating sandwiches, and having drinks, more jovial and less anxious than when they first arrived. Like they'd proven something that they'd set out to prove.

To Bill Allen and Dave Wills, two gun enthusiasts who also hunt a great deal, guns are works of art. They are for collecting and using and for taking fine care of.

Dave Wills is described by his good friend Bill as "The best stock maker in the whole country."

Dave, who is a big burly man with a salt and pepper beard, tried to make his living as a full-time gunsmith once, but gave it up when he realized that he could make as much money being a grill cook at McDonald's. Nevertheless, gunsmithing is in Dave's genes, as he says, because his grandfather, whom he never met, was a blacksmith and gunsmith, too. All his life. It must have been more profitable back then.

Bill Allen is a clean-cut, youngish man, who recently retired from the military. His interest in guns lies in their history, in the story they could tell if they could talk. Bill has over 5,000 magazines and catalogues from years gone by that describe all kinds of guns.

The magazines cover guns made anywhere from the Turn of the Century to World War II. Bill and Dave call this the "Golden Age of Gun Making and Hunting."

That's because guns were then made by hand. They were of a better quality. As for hunting, there were no game limits, no seasonal limits and no end to the amount of land available for hunting.

Both Dave and Bill own some pretty old, pretty valuable guns. But they just don't display them at shows. They shoot them, too.

"Taking a high-quality gun on a hunt is the beauty of it," says Bill.

"Buying a great gun and then not shooting it is like buying a Mercedes and then not driving it."

Both men are primarily bird hunters. Quail and dove. They think certain deer hunters are, well, unsophisticated, to put it mildly.

"Guns are just tools to a lot of the deer hunters I know," Bill says. "To me, a gun is a work of art."

And Bill and Dave haven't just come to the conclusion that guns are fascinating studies. They were both brought up with guns and hunting. They're oldtimers.

"It's the history of the gun that fascinates me," says Dave. "To think that this gun you're holding was used to fight Indians, or in the Civil War is just so interesting to me, personally."

Dave and Bill go to a lot of these gun shows that are held on Saturdays. At the shows, people show off their collections and swap guns with each other and sell to each other.

But despite their love of guns and their love of their beauty, their history and their quality, and despite their great love of hunting in the great outdoors, both will tell you very readily that shooting a gun at some animal in the woods is a very small part of what they find attractive about hunting. Even these guys will tell you there is a lot more to hunting than pulling the trigger of a $5,000 shotgun. That's not to say that pulling the trigger isn't fun. It's saying that it's just not a big thing if they don't get a shot off. And these guys have been hunting for a long time. They should know what is fun and what is not fun about hunting.

"Eventually," says Bill, "you get to the point where killing isn't the most important part of the hunt. It's secondary, it really is."

"Yeah, me and Dave know this fellow who lives down the street from me," Bill says. "He's got a fancy four-wheel-drive, one of those big, nice portable deer stands. He's got every kind of equipment he could ever want or need, and he hasn't got a shot off all season. He just hasn't got any luck."

How this would amuse the purple phantom.

THE DOGS

The most remarkable thing found in a grocery store these days is the magazine rack near the check-out stand.

Not only are most of these trendy magazines able to come up with zany new ways to generalize mankind each month, they continue to make millions simply by printing the word "New!" liberally on their covers.

Unsuspecting shoppers waiting for their frozen pizzas and panty hose to slide across the laser beam see it all the time—these magazines and their headlines. Ones that tell us how senior citizens are now incredibly active; how divorced mothers are now incredibly career oriented; how babies are now incredibly intelligent; how people who exercise are now incredibly healthy; and how fat people who have dieted are now incredibly thin. Of course, there's nothing incredibly "New!" about any of this. But that's the magazine business. If you believe in the revelations of their heavily punctuated headlines, you will believe that the decade of the 80s is the first decade in history during which women have held jobs and raised children, at the same time.

As far as revelations about men, at least half of these grocery store magazines, at one time or another, have done the "New Sensitive Males of the 80s" article. Usually featuring either Alan Alda or Phil Donahue. The magazines would have you believe that these new "sensitive" types are the first and only men in America able and unashamed to cry. But that's not so.

For instance, a good hunting dog—a real good hunting dog—can make any hunting man cry. Always could. And that hunter may never have even seen an episode of Donahue.

Take the case of 8 Ball and his owner, a dentist who hunted every chance he got. 8 Ball was what hunters refer to as a "real fine dog." And he was. Some say he was a descendent of another "real fine dog" named

Palamonium. But Palamonium was more than a fine dog, some say he was "the greatest (bird) dog that ever lived." But this is not the story of the greatest bird dog that ever lived, this is the story of a plain old every-day real fine dog, and his name was 8 Ball.

Now 8 Ball was a liver and white pointer who was given as a gift to the dentist by a generous dental colleague some years back.

That hunting dentist loved 8 Ball right from the start. That's because 8 Ball loved to hunt as much as his master and because he was very good at it. He never ran up a covey of quail in his entire abbreviated life, even though he found quite a few. He always honored the points of other dogs, which is proper etiquette for bird dogs. He even got along nicely with his master's family, and that was a real bonus. No man could ask for more in a bird dog. And no man ever did.

More than one of the dentist's hunting partners offered money for 8 Ball. But the dentist wouldn't hear of selling him. Not a chance. That dentist was going to hang on to his 8 Ball. Mere money would be a poor substitute for the joy, pride and weekly ego boost he derived from being the owner of that dog. Kept his freezer full of quail, too.

"That sure is a fine dog you got there," the other hunters would say to him. "Yes sir-eee, that there is a real fine dog."

And 8 Ball continued to live up to his growing reputation until one day, somewhere out in the country, 8 Ball made the fatal mistake of romping across an old dirt road without first stopping to look both ways. Cut down, he was, in the prime of his life, by a soybean farmer in a big hurry to get to town.

That was the end of 8 Ball. A dog to be proud of.

Several months later, that same dentist was attending one of those functions only a dentist could love. It was a meeting of the state dental association. And as scores of dentists and their wives mixed and mingled and made small talk about things such as tartar control, the dentist chanced to meet the kind dentist friend who had given him 8 Ball in the first place.

Being a big hunter himself, and because he had known how good a dog 8 Ball was, the unsuspecting dentist friend just naturally greeted his colleague with the obvious question: "How's old 8 Ball doing? Y'all finding any quail?"

The dentist didn't answer the question right away. Instead, he began a thorough sight inspection of the tops of his white bucks.

Silence.

The puzzled dentist who'd asked the question stood there uneasily waiting for what he thought should have been a relatively simple answer.

More silence.

Then, slowly and not very distinguishable at first, tiny pools of salty liquid began forming in the blue eyes of 8 Ball's former owner. Then, as the dentist friend looked on in amazement, those tiny pools became droplets. And those droplets began running down the face of his forlorn colleague and he began to cry. To sob, actually, right there in the middle of all those chattering dentists and their wives. A few of them stopped in mid-sentence and glanced curiously in the crying man's direction.

The surprised dentist friend looked first toward the left, then toward the right. He placed a tentative, but comforting hand on the wailing dentist's shoulder.

"What is it?" he asked timidly.

"8 Ball's de . . . he's dead!

A good hunting dog, a real fine dog, has that kind of effect on a man, sensitive or otherwise.

"There used to be a piece of land, about 1,500 acres out there by the airport. Kenny used to come out there every other Sunday wanting to quail hunt, and we had a lot of birds. And he come out there one day and said, 'Y'all want to go quail hunting?' And we said, 'Yeah, we'll go.' And he said he had a pretty good dog and I said, 'Yeah, well how 'bout letting me bring my own dog,' and he said, 'Will he back? Is he a good dog?' And I said, 'Yeah, he's a good dog.'

"So we went out there and his dog was real fancy and wide ranging and my dog disappeared. His dog went and found a covey of birds and pointed.

"'Where's your dog?' And I said, 'He's around here somewhere.' And he said, 'Will he back?' And I said, 'I told you once, he's a good dog.' Well, we shot that covey of birds and still I didn't have my dog.'

"'Where's your dog?' And I told him, 'He's out there on a covey of birds.' He said, 'He can't be, we've been shooting.' And I said, 'That don't make any difference.' And he said, 'What are you talking about?' And I said, 'If he's out there on a covey of birds, he ain't gonna move.'

"And this was true.

"So we started looking for him and I walked about two or three hundred yards and I saw him, about half lying down, pointing, and I said, 'He's got a covey of birds.' And Kenny said, 'It can't be. I never saw a dog keep a point that long.' And I said, 'If you'd been shot as many times as he had, you'd do it too.' So we eased up there and I said, 'Go ahead.' And we walked up about a hundred yards and after a few minutes, I saw him look around toward me and I said, 'Will your dog back?' And he said, 'If he don't, I'll kill him.'

Of course, you shouldn't start to think that it's just the bird dogs who exert strong emotional tugs on the heart strings of their owners. For there are other fine hunting dogs to consider. Dogs who are revered not for their abilities to point and stand and honor, but for their abilities to do other things, like track and tree and howl.

These are the coon dogs. Maybe they're not as pretty to watch as are the pointers and setters. Maybe they're not as graceful. But you can say one thing about them that can't be said of dogs like 8 Ball. In the South, coon dogs have their own official burying ground. A graveyard where the best of them are laid to rest in heavenly peace. And where their former masters come to pay their respects from time to time.

No, you can't say there is anything to compare with what is done for the best of the South's coon dogs. And if you have never had a coon dog to call your own, and if you've never hunted him through swamps and brush and muck in the dead of night, you might not even understand a thing like a coon dog graveyard. And the thing is, no one cares if

you don't.

"I went coon hunting with three of the darndest coon hunters you've ever seen. They had the headlights on their caps and their hip boots on. They weren't serious. They were seerus. And they had three black-and-tan hounds that must have weighed 100 pounds apiece. And man when they hit a coon, they could sing. They got that coon up a tree and they climbed about 10 feet up the tree and they got so mad they started chewing the bark off the tree. It looked like a beaver had been there. One of these dogs was the state coon dog champion two out of the last three years. And we were hunting down there around Sawyerville, on the edge of the river. And the coon went across the river, big wide water, and that dog followed that coon across and treed him on the other side. And we could see it with the lights, see the dog and see the coon. And these guys got back in the truck and went back up and crossed the river up there at Ackland, went back into Eutaw and down, back on the backside of Dollarhyde. An hour and a half it took them to get there, and that dog was still treeing that coon. An hour and a half! And one of the men said if they hadn't gone to get him, he'd have just stayed there."

Key Underwood didn't train the dog, he didn't even see the dog's best years, but Underwood was the man who buried the dog and that made the difference.

It is Labor Day and there's a party at the graveyard—the Key Underwood Coon Dog Memorial Graveyard—in the Freedom Hills. The annual celebration on this muggy September afternoon honors over 150 black-and-tans, redbones, blueticks and other hounds who rest beneath rustic markers bearing names, dates and passages of praise, such as the salute worn by "Bragg: The Best East of the Mississippi River," and "Rusty—A Coon Dog Indeed."

Never mind the storm. It looms to the east, dark, big, but in no hurry, and so the storm is braved as are the winding back roads the celebrants have travelled upon to get here.

The atmosphere is friendly and buzzing, with so many familiar faces in one place. The sound of bluegrass music and the smell of barbecue stir the senses. An old man with a long white beard and a Mack Truck cap buck dances with his grandchildren.

The women tap their feet as they converse from their lawn chairs placed just outside the picnic shed. The men drift and huddle about the grounds. They are members of the Tennessee Valley Coon Dog Hunter's Association, host of the affair and overseer of the 10-acre tract of backwoods land. The membership of the club has dwindled to 40 in recent years, and many of that number have aged beyond coon chasing.

"Hey, Sheriff, over here!" calls a husky gentleman leaning against a pine tree and wearing a USMC baseball cap. A tiny American flag on a toothpick sticks out of his shirt pocket. His face is red and wrinkled like the palm of a working man's hand. His cheek is swollen with tobacco, and his clothes are old and stained.

The sheriff, a tall thin man, his revolver tucked down between the front of his pants and his stomach, moves hurriedly over. "What can I do for you, suh?" he asks, shaking hands.

The heavy man, his weight still against the tree, speaks with a frog in his throat. "Sheriff, what are we gonna do 'bout this vandalism goin' on 'round here? Maybe we ought to get a sign put up or somethin'?"

The sheriff stares down at the ground and rubs his chin. His face shows genuine concern, as if he's trying to decide right now what should be done about the vandalism. The ex-marine looks down, too, with the same concern, as if he and the sheriff are working on this problem together; as if to say to everyone around them, "Y'all go on and have fun. Me and the sheriff's gonna work it out."

The Hunt

The systematic search for raccoons does not begin until the last crimson ray of sunlight has dissolved in the western, winter sky. It is a frigid night. A night not cold enough to freeze the water on the ground, but one with just enough steely moisture in the air to make it miserable. It's a Deep South cold that penetrates the clothing and the skin and the bones. And it's dark. Pitch dark. The moon is eclipsed by a heavy cloud cover. With no lights on, you can barely make out the foursome of men standing alongside their pick-ups. They are situated in a muddy, fallow field, on the edge of a big swamp. A sure enough, dense-as-dirt, slimy Southern swamp.

Some coon hunters prefer a full moon. But Larry says it doesn't matter. If the coons are out there, the dogs will find them. After all, Bill is here. And Bill is the state coon dog champion.

Bill and four other black-and-tan hounds like himself are kept secured in dog boxes in the beds of the trucks. The dogs are whining with anticipation.

"Hush down in there!" one of the men shouts over at the boxes. But the command is not enough to quell the whines of the impatient hounds. In fact, it only makes them grow louder. Did the hunter know it would? Was that his way of joining in the dogs' anxious rumblings? If there were any light out here tonight the others might have seen the glint of teeth, the hint of a smile on their companion's lips. He's not interested in silencing the dogs, then. He's only sharing their sentiments. If he were one of the dogs, he'd be whining, too. But he's not, he's a man, so he must use words.

Coon hunting is as old as farming in the South. It was born out of a need to protect crops from these hungry little nighttime burglars. They especially liked to eat corn crops, and still do, but farmers couldn't have that, so they started hunting them down, and after a time, it became sport. Like tonight.

After a few more apprehensive moments, the dogs are let loose into the swamp, their noses to the ground. Larry says coons are found best around water, because they have poor salivary glands. Coons don't really wash their little hands before eating, as you are told in kindergarten. Rather, they soak their food in the water—wet it up good—so they can swallow it.

The foursome can hear the dogs splashing through the water and kicking up leaves—then the sounds fade away into the black depths of the swamp.

Meanwhile, the men are getting their gear ready in silence. They are listening out for the dogs, keeping one ear turned toward the swamp as they affix their coal mining-like helmets on their heads. They clip their leashes on their pants. One of them checks out a .22 rifle, another packs tobacco in his mouth. Even with this cold, no one takes a drink of whiskey. These are pros, not good ole boys out for a night of boozing.

By and by the dogs can be heard again. This time, it's not their movement, but their baying that breaks the silence. The men know pretty much—or pretend to know—which sound belongs to which dog. Bill's voice is the most distinguishable, a guttural hoooowwwww-hoooowwwww-hoooowwwww. He's on a scent. And the other dogs have joined his frenzied chant. Soon the men know the dogs have found and treed a coon.

"Sounds 'bout a quarter mile away," one of them says, and as if on cue, all of them cross over the barbed wire fence that separates the field from the swamp and take out after the dogs through the black mire.

Hot-footing it through a grimy swamp in the middle of the night in single-minded pursuit of baying hounds must be very similar to being part of a sheriff's posse in pursuit of a fleeing convict.

There is very little talking during this fast-paced trek through the mud except for occasional directives such as, "This way!" and "Over yonder!"

No one cares during this race to the tree about football scores, frozen feet or new fissures in Mount St. Helens. Because for a time, there are no such things. There is only one thing. The dogs. Where they are. What they've got. Who'll get there first.

These men don't actually run—it would be too difficult. They take long, quick strides like athletes in a walking race. A walking race through five inches of muck.

Waist-high rubber boots keep the water away from their feet, and fill the dark swamp with sounds of Schluk, Schluk, Schluk as they trod through the sticky ooze.

Soon, the sounds of the dogs get louder. "Here they are!" shouts one of the hunters. And sure enough, as the lights of the helmets are shined on them, the dogs can be seen; barking and baying as if possessed. They are trying to climb up the tree, but with all their clawing and climbing, can only make it a few feet up the trunk. Things quiet down a little as each man collars his hound and pulls him back. A host of bright lights illuminate the limbs of the tree, about three or four stories up. It takes a minute for the hunters to locate their prey.

And there, finally, just barely visible, is the coon. He is clinging to a limb for all he is worth. One of the men puts a coon call into his mouth and blows—Grrrr, Grrrrr, Grrrrr. The object of this is to make the coon look down toward that sound, so his eyes will reflect the light of the beams, and he can be seen more easily.

The coon falls for this trick and looks down, his eyes shining brightly against his dark face, against the dark of the night. His curious, terrified eyes are his downfall.

In the old days, it is said, coon hunters would simply cut down the tree to get the coon to the ground. But now, with the price of timber what it is, most landowners frown on that sort of thing.

So the accepted modern way to get at the coon is to shoot him down. One of the men puts the rifle to his shoulder and fires. The dogs whine in ecstasy.

"Missed him," another man says. So the fellow shoots again. This time the shot finds its mark.

"Watch your head!" someone shouts, as the coon, drunkenly, loses his grip on the branch and begins to fall, almost in slow motion at first. He glances off a branch just below him, reaches out a clumsy paw to catch himself, but fails. About halfway down the tree the fall seems to gain momentum. A split second later the coon lands with a dull thud on the damp ground. Watching this scene is like seeing one of those natives who takes a dive from a tall tree with a rope tied to his leg. Only nothing stops the coon from smacking the dirt.

After hitting the ground, the coon, stunned, begins a feeble attempt to crawl away. A couple of the men let their dogs inch up to where the coon is lying. They hold the dogs' collars as they allow them to snatch the coon up into their mouths, and shake it to and fro. It's not much of a fight. After a few minutes, they pull the dogs back. They don't want the coon for eating, but they do have plans to sell the skins, so they don't want to mess it up too bad with teeth marks and tears.

"Dead coon!" they holler at the dogs to calm them down. "Dead coon! Come on now! Dead coon!"

And they are right.

Then the caravan of men and hounds crosses back through the swamp and the barbed wire. The dead coon is tossed in the back of one of the trucks and the gentlemen start their engines and move about 100 yards on down the field. The dogs are let loose again. The process is repeated.

Two hours later, the men have five coons to their credit. It is a good night for the hunt.

Now, coon hunting doesn't seem to require the skills of many other types of hunting. As Larry says, "The dogs do all the work." But these men are as serious, and as intent as any turkey hunter to succeed. It's that seriousness, that intent, that keeps conversation to a minimum. You won't hear many jokes, many anecdotes in the company of this bunch.

Between coons, the men wait. Leaned up against trees or a truck. For minutes at a time, often, the only sound to be heard is of someone spitting. Of someone spitting and of that same spit hitting the ground. It's quiet.

"There goes Joe," one man says, finally, upon hearing a low baying off in the swamp.

"No it ain't," says another. "That's Misty. That's your little ole puppy."

"No it ain't."

"Yeah it is."

Another man joins the discussion. "Yeah it is, too."

"Well if it is, she got two mouths, then," Misty's owner replies a bit defensively.

"That's Misty."

"Sure as hell is."

"Yeah?"

Silence.

"Maybe it is."

Another voice joins Misty's disputed one.

"There goes Joe," one of them says.

"Where the hell is Bill?"

"He'll be along," says Bill's owner.

Silence. More spitting.

"Yeah, there's Bill."

Conversations as animated and in-depth as these continue throughout the night, culminating in the final scene at the tree. The shot. The fall. The kill. The back tracking to the truck.

Once during the night, the dogs are able to tree three coons at one time, only the hunters cannot manage to kill but one. The tree is too tall and branchy. Two coons escape with their skins, but before the hunters will concede this defeat, they stand, staring up at the tree for a long, long time, with their lights dancing in and around the thick branches. They're not happy about losing these two at all.

"I've been hunting since I was this high," says Larry, holding his hand around his hip. "I just grew up with it."

The others with Larry probably did, too, only they don't volunteer this information. Mostly they are silent, except to talk about the hounds. It's not what you'd call a happy-go-lucky bunch. But then, they are not here to socialize. They are here to work the hounds. And so deep is their concentration as they sit listening for their hounds, you have to wonder to what extent the success of these dogs relates to their own, as men. Surely one has nothing to do with the other. Surely it's just the darkness. The silence. The cold, clammy imaginings that emanate from this old swamp that set the mind to such extrinsic wonderings. It is not possible for the observer to keep interest in the far off howling of the hounds, though. So the observer must think of something else. Remember, there is no talking. Every attempt at conversation has been nipped in the bud. And it is either thoughts of these men or of this swamp that must occupy the mind. The swamp. Like a living graveyard. Eery to the senses. Thoughts of murder and hatchet men from summer camp stories told fireside fill the head. It is more soothing to think about the men.

Like the two coons who got away, this is their escape, this hunting in the middle of the night in the middle of nowhere. This is their flight from time clocks and monthly mortgage payments and domestic drudgery. This is their fun.

It is not difficult for the first-time coon hunter to grasp the basic concept of the sport, even during the first 5 minutes, if a coon is found during that span of time. But a love, a true love of this game, this hunt, must take time. It must. Because coon hunting is not the sort of thing a person just warms up to right away, like a sheep dog puppy. In fact, it's kind of shocking. Raw.

In duck hunting, you get to see the sun rise over a secluded river or pond some-where. In turkey hunting, you sit in the deep woods and see if you can talk to one of God's creatures. Even on a dove hunt, you can swap gossip with fellow hunters on a pleasant afternoon in the country. But coon hunting is neither a social event (not this one, anyway) nor a scenic tour of nature's beauty (you can barely see your hand in front of your face). Coon hunting involves a sometimes viscious torturing of the prey when it doesn't have to, and a first-time observer of this sport is likely to feel a little sorry for the coon. After all, most Americans are brought up to respect this clean-living little creature with the cute mask. And on those occasions when the coon gets away from the pack of hounds and hunters who urge them on, the first-time observer is likely to feel a secret sense of relief.

And if this observer is between the age of, say 25 and 40, then something rather peculiar might be going on in his or her head as the group heads out to yet another kill at the tree.

". . . Rocky Raccoon, checked into his room, only to find Gideon's Bible . . ."

The sheriff looks up at the sky and folds his arms. "I think sometimes it's best not to advertise the situation," he says. "Puttin' up a sign that says not to do somethin' only entices more of 'em to do it. I'm 'fraid that's how it works sometimes."

The heavy fella nods his head slowly in agreement and spits tobacco at another pine tree nearby, missing. "Guess you're right," he mumbles.

The sheriff pats him on the shoulder and moves into the crowd, shaking hands as he goes.

The cemetery, though only yards from the activity around the shed, still possesses a respectful isolation. As the coon hunters gather at the stones of Old Red, Beanblossom Bommer and Miller's Blue, there is admiration and pride and humor in their yarns about these glorious coon hounds of yesteryear taking on the gritty raccoon. But then silence creeps gently into the air. Their eyes stare longingly at the graves. Perhaps, their sudden melancholy is a result of mourning the dogs, and perhaps it's a result of mourning their own youth, buried, it seems, with the dogs.

"Heck, I wore all my old huntin' buddies out," says an old gentleman scanning the graveyard as he leans against a table underneath the shed.

"Guess I ran 'em too hard. I had to give it up a couple years ago myself, but I outlasted all of 'em."

"Bet you were climbin' trees 'til the end," a young listener speculates.

"No, sir," the man says assuredly. "How do you think I made it long as I did? I gave up climbin' in the late 30s. See, one night a dog treed a coon up a big ole tall hickory tree. Coon went way up yonder. I told the boys I'd get that coon out of there real smart like and I took off my jacket and climbed and climbed and got to the top and there he was. I teased him a little and he jumped out and the dogs caught him. Well, I looked around and I could see the lights in Tuscumbia and Cherokee and I got this feelin' come over me said you're a lot higher than you oughta be. Said you're dangerously high. Next thing I was thankin' the good Lord for lookin' after me while I climbed up that tree, and I told Him that if He let me get back down without fallin' that I'd never climb another one. Well I made it back down and I never did climb another."

The old man speaking is the supreme veteran of the club, 85-year-old Key Underwood. He is a small, thin man with glasses and very large ears. His nose runs crooked into a cherry tip. His flesh sags with age at the chin and neck, but his complexion holds a healthy color. He wears a baggy, gray short-sleeved shirt and slacks, and on his head is the obligatory baseball cap. His says "Key Underwood Coon Dog Memorial Graveyard". The cap sells for $5 at this event every year.

Key Underwood buried the first dog here Labor Day Eve in 1937. That dog was named Troop, a renowned coon racer and fighter in his day who has earned legendary status since his death, at least in local coon hunting circles.

Someone asks Underwood to tell his famous story. He obliges without hesitation. His voice is soft and country.

"First of all, I didn't train that dog," he says. "Old whiskey maker trained that dog. But when the revenue man caught him, his wife was left with the dog and she pawned him to a man named Childers. I went over there to look this fella up and see what he would take for the dog and ended up payin' him $75. That was 1932. Troop was already 10 years old."

Asked what kind of dog Troop was, Underwood squints and thinks a moment and shrugs. "I don't remember what kind. He was a big dog. A red and white spotted dog. He was poor looking and skinny when I bought him. No, I don't remember what kind. I don't remember things like I used to. Sometimes I even get my stories mixed up."

Underwood removes his glasses and wipes them slowly. "But I do remember the first time I took old Troop out. I was with a couple other boys. Troop cold-trailed for an hour and a half and every time he'd bark those boys wanted to go to him. But I told 'em to hold on, to give Troop some time. Then that dog came back on a tree and froze on it. One of the boys didn't believe there was a coon up there, but I saw it was hollow and thought we oughta cut it down. We all carried axes back then. So we went at it. Took about 30 minutes for that tree to fall. Then I turned old Troop loose. First he circles the tip of the tree but there's no coon.

Then he goes down to the butt of the tree and here comes the coon outa there practically runnin' over me. Well Troop's movin' like a bull yearlin' when he gets to that coon and he knocks him down. Then Troop lets up and starts walkin' and sniffin' around the coon and that nasty coon's squallin' back at Troop. I said to myself this dog's not gonna kill this coon, he's afraid of him. Maybe Troop isn't such a good coon dog after all. But old Troop was just waitin' on the coon to start runnin' again. Sure enough that coon takes off and Troop catches him from behind by the shoulder, rams him down on the ground, and that was it.

"I saw then, I had a good dog."

Underwood says he's owned eight to 10 good coon dogs during his life, but never one that could beat his Troop. "That Troop was a professional. He didn't have any bad habits. He didn't growl at other dogs. He had a good nose. I saw him do things a dog just can't do."

Underwood puts on his glasses and nods. "Yessir, I had five good years with Troop. But the day came where he couldn't eat or get up. I had a vet put him to sleep. After it was done, I called up the boys and one of 'em said Troop deserved a decent burial bein' he was such a good dog. Well, we had always camped and hunted around here so we carried Troop on out."

What Underwood did next, on the night of Troop's death—Labor Day Eve, nearly a half-century ago—protrudes from the Earth 10 yards from where Underwood stands. It is a modest piece of chimney rock, and chiseled into it is a tiny cross, the name, "Troop", and the dates of Troop's birth, 4-1-22, and death, 9-4-37.

Of course, Underwood didn't realize he had founded a coon dog cemetery in 1937. He was simply burying his favorite dog. But in the years that followed, a few of his friends so honored their hounds as well. Underwood became cemetery caretaker in his spare time. Deceased hounds began to arrive from Alabama, Tennessee, Mississippi and Kentucky. And Key Underwood, a former hardware store employee, described by a club acquaintance as a good, common, moral man, soon found himself and his cemetery featured on national television and in a national magazine.

136

"Let's eat 'fore the rain comes!" cries a female voice from the tables.

A long line forms quickly. Underwood stands in the middle observing the faces around him. He acknowledges several with a smile and a wave. He is feeling good today because his story is the reason they've come together. He hopes his story will continue to bring them here, long after he's gone.

"One afternoon I was hunting with Max, and it was getting into late after-noon. It was back when there was still a lot of open land to hunt on and there were a lot of birds. We were hunting with both our dogs, and we find this covey and flush it up and we both kill several birds. So my dog goes out there to retrieve and he picks one up in his mouth, and on his way back he runs across another bird lying there, and he picks that one up, too, so he brings me back two birds at once. We keep hunting and after a while we run up on another covey and flush it and I think we each killed one out of that covey. So my dog goes out there and picks up one of the birds and as he's coming back with the bird in his mouth, he comes across a bird that hasn't gotten up yet, and that dog stood there and pointed that bird with a bird in his mouth. Now that was something. I had another dog, Joe, who was potentially the best dog I ever had. And I took Joe out as a puppy one time, just showing him the ropes and teaching him, and he found three coveys of birds that day. Just a puppy!

"But then my wife and I went to Miami and while we were gone, one of my kids let Joe out of the pen and he got run over by a car. After he got better from the accident he could still hunt and find birds, but I never could make him mind very well, like he did before he got hit. I think that car smack-ing into him kind of addled his brain. He would have been a real fine dog except for that."

A man like Key Underwood wouldn't pay much attention to what goes on from time to time at Sedgefields Plantation, a land lover's retreat deep in the heart of Dixie. It's so Southern around these parts that local cafes serve grits automatically with any breakfast because they wouldn't imagine anyone could eat a breakfast without them.

But Underwood wouldn't care about Sedgefields, because it's a place dedicated to bird dogs. Coon dogs take a rear seat.

In fact, Sedgefields Plantation is where the cream of the quail dog lineage gathers for what insiders call "The Kentucky Derby" of the bird dog world.

Sedgefields is where the National Free-for-all Birddog Championships are held, and on a relentlessly hot day in February, dog men from Minnesota to Texas and many places in between are gathered for the three-week-long event, to see whose dog among them will be the best at finding the quail.

Pete Thuman, a dog trainer at the Sundown Kennels in Texas, is among the participants. He hasn't come all this way for the prize money, heaven knows. The winner of the derby trials for two-year-olds gets $1,500 and the winner of the free-for-all, held for dogs of all ages, will get $5,000. Pete Thuman and his assistant, David, come for the chance to win and build their reputations as dog trainers of merit. If the money is to ever come, it will come after a trainer has established himself. Some men have been known to pay as much as $24,000 for a good quail dog. Some even more.

Along with men like Pete, are the socially prominent ladies and gentlemen who have been fortunate enough to garner an invitation from the plantation's owner, Jimmy Hinton. These men and women do not attend because of any burning desire to see a particular dog win, but because they enjoy spending the afternoon on horseback in the company of other socially acceptable people like themselves. These revelers will follow the trial course along behind the ones in the running for the championship.

Among them is a young lady by the name of Olivia, whose family lives on what 150 years ago would have been called a "neighboring planta-tion." It's just a big house now, surrounded by fields. They don't call them plantations anymore, unless it's part of the formal name, like Sedgefields Plantation.

Olivia is a vivacious and attractive brunette; an art major, who has come here to Sedgefields today with her mother, sister, and horse.

It's an interesting mix of people. There are the dog trainers like Pete—with his scuffed cowboy boots, faded Levi's and belt buckle the size of a salad plate—who spend the time between heats taking cat naps in the backs of horse trailers, watering their dogs or just sitting. And there are the people like Olivia, who spend the time between heats sipping light beer and chatting in animated fashion with each other. This is a party to them. This is work to the others.

There are maybe 140 dogs entered in the trial, and they compete two at the time. On this particular day, dog trainers and horse trainers and party guests begin arriving at the plantation stables and club house early in the morning.

Those interested mainly in riding their horses are pleased with the un-expected early spring that has bathed Sedgefields in a brilliant light and is causing little beads of sweat to form on the upper parts of their socially tactful, skillfully conversing lips. "Can you imagine it being so beautiful right here at the first of February?" they ask each other. "I never dreamed I'd need my sun block this time of the year," they say. "I do believe we're all going to blister."

Meanwhile, the dog trainers, who've come all this way and paid all this money in gas and motel bills, are grumbling. "It's gonna be hell trying to find the birds today," they mutter. "Too damn hot. Too damn dry."

Hot or not, birds or no birds, the field trials will go on. You don't call the Kentucky Derby on account of a little good weather.

Just before the first two contenders are let loose on their hour-and-a-half course, those involved in the trials busy themselves saddling and bridling their mounts. Some show signs of lather on this merciless February day, from earlier romps around the course.

The "circuit" is the various dog trial events held all across the U.S. and Canada during the course of the year. It's like the pro tennis circuit, only you won't catch anyone wearing white shorts, and there's not near the money to be won.

The next heat is to begin at 1 p.m. and it is right around that time that the 30 or so observers on horseback begin to assemble at the rear of the clubhouse. The course the two dogs will traverse for the next 90 minutes is, at the start, about as wide as one side of an interstate highway. It gets more narrow and rugged in places and in other areas it spreads out to the width of a football field. Some of the more far-sighted riders put beers in their saddle bags, while others do well just to keep their spirited mounts in check.

The two dog handlers ride ahead of the pack as the dogs are let loose upon the rolling hills and wooded expanses of the Sedgefields Plantation. And a few minutes later, the pack of riders begins its journey at a slow jog. It rarely gets any faster than this. The dogs are not in sight

of the observing horseback riders for more than a minute or so at the time, because they are busy up ahead in the brush, looking for the quail that many say will not be found on a day like this one. Too damn hot and dry.

You have to wonder then, since the horseback riders don't see that much of the dogs, why they took such pains to get here. Couldn't they have had as much fun on a regular old trail ride? Probably not. For there is action here. Something is being accomplished. There's an element of surprise and anticipation in the air. And these riders, these southern folk with their horses, are a part of that action, a very hot, very slow Southern kind of action, that links them to their Southern heritage and allows them to live it.

The only ones taking great pains to keep up with the dogs are the handlers, the scouts and the judges, who are seen passing back and forth across the course from time to time.

Every so often, the dogs scare up small groups of deer, and the riders ooh and aah at the sight of them springing through the woods. The dogs, though, don't pay the deer any attention. They know better.

The last brace of the day is over, and most everyone is back at the stables, preparing to head out. The sun is just beginning to set, and the heat of the day is quickly losing its grip.

Leaving the Sedgefields Plantation at twilight, a visitor gets a good look at the amber fields and woodlands that make up this uncommonly peaceful expanse of land and wonders if the horses, dogs, wildlife and handful of people who live here know just how good they have it. There aren't that many places like this left in the South.

Meanwhile, back at the stables, Pete and his hand, David, are wrapping things up for the day. It's been a pretty good one, not because they won anything, but because they sold a dog.

There are some who say dog trainers are like used car salesmen. That an honest one is wonderful and difficult to find. And that many of them will tell you the merchandise is in top condition before you buy it, but when you get home with it you find out differently. Pete, though, doesn't strike you as a man who would swindle you. Just a man doing the best he can with what he's got.

Just listen to a group of hunters sometime, as they are sitting around rehashing the events of previous hunts, and you're going to hear a dog story or two. Maybe some of the stories have improved with age, and maybe some of them have lost a little in the translation. But a hunter who loves dogs is going to tell them just the same, because working with the dogs is what makes the hunting such a pleasure to him. And remembering the feats of dogs past is what makes the memory of the hunt all the more special.

The vast majority of bird dogs, deer dogs and coon dogs will never be honored with a headstone after their deaths like at Key Underwood's coon dog graveyard. And the bulk of them will never be good enough to enter—much less win—the field trials at Sedgefields. Most will just hunt, and when they're too old to hunt, they'll be left behind.

But in the backseat of a car traveling somewhere, or on the church steps, or in front of a fire in a ramshackle old hunting lodge in the woods, those old dogs and those long dead will live to hunt again in the telling of their stories. And their stories will bring smiles to the faces of the story tellers, and many times, even tears.

A good dog, a "real fine dog," has that kind of effect on most hunters. And perhaps even the most moved among them could never tell you why that is so.

THE HUNTER

Take a man born and raised in Atlanta, who never traveled beyond its suburbs, who saw deer only on television, who never held a gun, and ask him if he is a hunter. He won't answer: I am not a hunter. He will say he has never hunted, but that he believes quite frankly he could master it in little time.

He will say he is a man of the outdoors. It is in his blood. Drop him off in the woods with a gun, and though he has never touched a gun nor stalked in the woods, he'll figure it out. This, at least, is what he dreams. And he will do little more than dream it.

But dreams are not good enough for many Southerners. They will go into the woods, not blindly, but with their fathers who know how to hunt and who teach them how to hunt, and then they, in turn, will accompany their sons into the woods and teach a new generation how to hunt. They are the real carriers of the torch and they will maintain a relationship with the outdoors and the South.

In the not so distant past, many Southerners could simply walk out of their front doors and start hunting. One could walk and hunt for weeks and months without brushing against too much civilization. The 20th Century hunter can't stay away that long, not only because he would lose his job and probably his wife, but because the land isn't so open for the hunter's picking as it was for his ancestors. Too may trespassing signs and too many cities would stall the hunter's expedition. What he can do, what he must do, is overcome a work week's worth of weariness, pack his car and tangle with the 20th Century phenomenon called traffic until he reaches another house, a lodge which is deep in the woods.

When he arrives at this house in the woods the worry of work suddenly disappears, the aches in his body subside, the sleepiness in his head

lifts. He becomes alive and vigorous. His is a total and marvelous transformation. Frequently the rendezvous at this house in the woods is with several other hunters, even dozens of hunters, who also became better men when their eyes fell upon this house. He and they lease this house and the land surrounding it. They call themselves a hunting club and they give their club a name.

Oftentimes, a member of the club is also the owner of the house and the land. If he is, it could be that his father or grandfather and their hunting companions built the house and founded the club. These older family houses are generally nicer than most one finds in the woods. They may be built of virgin cypress, with a spacious dining area, a fully equipped kitchen, two sleeping rooms, a couple of fireplaces and a screened-in porch looking out at the river or over the mountains. It could be the club allows membership into this house only to the sons and grandsons of the founders. These older clubs drip with tradition. It is in the photos covering the walls of hunts and hunters past—of men cutting other men's shirttails because of a lousy shot, of a bloodied face after a first kill, of grandfather, father and son kneeling behind three dead buck. It is in the

young man learning from his elders how to dress, when to shut up, when to talk, how to drink. It is in the respect received by senior club members, the kind of respect once reserved for Confederate Generals.

It is in the huntmaster's drawl, which seems to stretch around the bend as he converses with fellow members gathering with shotguns in hand at sunrise for a deer drive. It is in the relationship with the black man, who is present to handle the dogs and to prepare the venison in the kitchen for lunch. It is the hunt itself. The Rules. The Dogs. The Grovers. The Shotguns. The Blood. The Death. It is in man's natural desire to prey. It is in the stories swapped late at night about the fireplace inside.

A man reaches down deep into his soul and pulls out raw manhood at the house in the woods. He shares this manhood with other men. He kills with them. He drinks with them. He cusses with them. He jokes with them. He reminisces into the morning hours with them. He is in a purely man's world. He won't find this world anywhere else. He is strong and confident and comfortable here. He doesn't want his liquor bottles

stationed behind the bar in the cabinet, he wants them in easy reach on top of the bar. He doesn't want his old hunting magazines tucked away, he prefers them piled up on the table in front of him. He desires no decorative touch to the hundreds of photos splattered on the walls.

He wishes the ashtray to remain on the arm of the chair forever. And, yes, that's his long underwear strewn about his unmade bed. He'll tidy up later; now it's time to eat. He is free to be a man here. He dives wholeheartedly into being one. If that means acting like a boy at times, so be it. But let a female crack this dome and the man shudders.

Let a woman walk into the midst of 30 men milling about their house in the woods and watch what happens. The 30 men don't ogle the woman or hoot or whistle or elbow each other in the ribs. They freeze. They absolutely freeze. Their immensely masculine state instantly drips with vulnerability. What is this creature come into our house in the woods? When their blood finally thaws somewhat they rise from their chairs and stagger into each other. One might speculate they are offering her a seat

in the name of chivalry and Rhett Butler. Hardly. They are moving away from her. They react with less terror over five charging boars. The man whom she has come to see is in the worst shape of all. He is sick with panic. He is the one who did not make it perfectly clear to his lady friend that she need not pay a visit to this house in the woods. His immediate duty is to get her out of there; preferably to drive her away so the others can quickly vote him out of the club.

At least, that's how some members in some of the clubs, particularly the older members in the older clubs, view the woman's intrusion. The wife of one of these members knows it's too late in the ballgame to

change her husband's ways; it's too late to become a partner in her husband's weekend excursions. She realizes she should have acted years ago. That very first weekend after the honeymoon as he packed his car to head out with the boys, she should have strutted out of the front door in full hunting attire and announced to him, "Let's get the show on the road, Jack." Maybe then it would have been different through the years. For 86-year-old Hazel Jones, speaking up early made all the difference in the world.

As eight men struggle out of their beds in the front room of a small house in the woods about a mile and a half north of the Tennessee River,

Hazel Jones, who slept alone in the back room where the kitchen and dining area are, and who awoke some time ago, scrambles eggs and heats biscuits. Near her on the wall are the words: A duck hunter is truth with frozen feet. Hazel Jones' feet, and the feet of the eight grumbling, scratching men hovering the fireplace in the front room, will be good and frozen about a half hour from now as they wait in blinds for the mallards and woodies to set their wings just above the Jones' 11 acre pond. Hazel Jones' late husband, Walter Jones, bought 150 acres flanked on two sides by the Wheeler Refuge in the late 50s. He chaperoned the heavy equipment crews required to get the pond just the way he wanted. Walter Jones is the reason Hazel has long been accustomed to rising in the cold darkness, cooking breakfast for a bunch of men, wading through broken ice and shooting ducks with her old lightweight 12 gauge Winchester.

"He was a determined hunter," Hazel says of her husband. "I learned early in my marriage that I would go with him or else I would be left at home."

Because she went with him, her memories of him are often linked with hunting. "I remember the day he had the Winchester delivered to me," she recalls. "We were getting ready to go down to our delta camp and it was delivered to me that morning. I had been using a 20 double barrel. You know I still have a callous on this finger from that gun. The Winchester is quite a bit lighter. The stock is all scarred and it practically got burned up two times in the truck, but I just feel so at home with it."

She is a small woman with twinkling eyes and good spirit, the way grandmothers should be. She does not surprise you when she says she collects duck feathers to make pillows for her grandchildren when they marry. She has spent many a day here in the pursuit of those feathers. She continues to host The Doctors' Club, a group of professionals and their families who've hunted here since long before Walter's death. "They were so afraid I wasn't going to keep it up," she says. "But they're still comin'."

Walter Jones did not limit his hunting to duck, which meant Hazel didn't either. She remains fond of turkey hunting and has killed five gobblers during her long life. She beams at the recollection of killing a gobbler her husband and several buddies had stalked at length in vain.

"We were down at a preserve," she says. "My husband and I used to go there year after year. I was under a power line next to a barbed wire fence, a good ways from where my husband and his friends were. An open field of wheat was all spread out before me. I saw the turkey on the other side of the fence. There came a chance when I got a good beat on that gobbler and I shot him. I don't know what I said, but I know I exclaimed. I don't think I was cussin', but I was so thankful. I crawled under the fence and I was just trembling. I could hardly lift that bird. He was a big one, 19 pounds. So I crawled back through the fence with my turkey and I sat back down and I was just so proud of myself. And after awhile here came my husband and his friends and one of them said, 'Mizz Hazel's done got our turkey'."

The men, including her son Doug, walk into the kitchen. Hazel greets them cheerfully as she runs warm water over their cold clean plates. She receives a chorus of thankyous for her hospitality. After breakfast, as she hides her tiny self inside her jacket and waders and picks up her Winchester, Hazel Jones says this has been a very happy place. She remembers when she and her husband and the dog would come out the first of the season and hunt two or three times a day; how she'd go in and get the mail and some groceries and he and the dog would stay; and eventually their friends would come out and then their boys . . .

Hazel Jones says she became a hunter to gain her husband's companionship. Her husband was a lucky man.

Hazel Jones is also an exception. Sure, more and more women hunt today in some of these larger clubs whose houses serve simply as a rendezvous point before the morning hunt, but don't look for too many women at the older tight-knit overnight clubs. Most women aren't willing to sleep in the back room while a dozen men walk around the front room in their long underwear.

Then again, there are some *men* who don't care about walking around the front room in their long underwear with a dozen other men. They can take or leave this house in the woods nonsense. They believe all that commotion merely takes the mind off the business at hand. They are the pure individuals of hunting. They are turkey hunters. They like to think of themselves as the intellectual element of hunting. No one is real certain why they think this way.

"I bet you before the deer season started Delchamps' stock went up three points cause there were guys walkin' the aisle and they were just loadin' stuff up to stock camp houses," says Tom Kelly, a turkey hunter. "And they love this and it's great. It keeps them out of the woods and they're not screwin' up dedicated turkey hunters who are out there doin' what God intended for them to do."

Again, no one understands why turkey hunters talk like this. Some say it's because they spend so much time alone in the woods. Others say they've developed an inferiority complex after years of being humiliated by the gobbler. A few theorize they got carried away by the scene in *Sergeant York*, when Gary Cooper in the heat of battle yelped a group of curious Germans out of their holes and then blasted them to pieces. The interesting thing is that turkey hunters believe in this "what God intended for them to do" kind of talk. Tom Kelly, for example, hides beneath the cloth of woodlands manager for a paper company, but everyone knows all he does is invite people into his office to talk turkey hunting, which Tom Kelly believes, really wholeheartedly believes, is the only hunting done on this earth that's worth a damn.

"Crops have been lost hunting turkeys and wives estranged. Fairly close relatives have gone into the grave at unattended funerals, except on extremely rainy days, and businesses have gone to rack and ruin unless sustained by sympathetic companions or associates who understand compulsions they do not share. I speak none of this in apologia, mind you. We need no apology. Subcultures exist in all societies."

The Hunt

Generally, a man does not take a rabbit hunt home with him. That is, he does not charge through his front door, immediately seek out his wife and lay upon her the exciting details of his pursuit of the hare. That's because a rabbit hunt is not very exciting; not very challenging either. It's one of those nice-to-be-outside hunts.

However, odds dictate that if a man goes on enough rabbit hunts in his life he is bound to engage something memorable.

About twice a year the owner invites a few locals over to hunt rabbits on his 3,000 acres. It's his way of offering a bit of his good fortune to those who want to hunt but don't have much of an opportunity now that land is tighter and hunting rights harder to come by. The owner's name is Mr. Downs, and on a bright, cool day in February Mr. Downs sits atop his white horse in front of the stable. Beside him on another horse is Mr. Thomas, a long-time friend and neighbor. Mr. Downs and Mr. Thomas are built quite alike. Both are tall with broad shoulders. Both have a full head of white hair as well. Mr. Downs wears long, thick sideburns while Mr. Thomas sports a beard cut neatly and close to his chin. He doesn't wear a mustache. Both have large noses, only Mr. Downs' nose is straight while Mr. Thomas' nose curves in three places. Mr. Thomas used to play football. Both men wear caps today. Both caps have the single letter "A" on them. Mr. Downs' "A" is red. Mr. Thomas' "A" is orange. Both wear sunglasses.

Beside Mr. Downs and Mr. Thomas stand two of the locals named Richard and Brent. They wear overalls and hold shotguns. Richard is a tall, muscular man and his skin shines under the sun. Brent is skinny and short and his overalls eat him up. Richard's face is strong with a wide flat nose and healthy cheeks. He hasn't shaved in a couple of days. Brent's face is weak with a thin nose and sunken cheeks. He hasn't shaved in a couple of days either. Both of these men also wear caps, only their caps have no lettering stitched on them. Richard's cap is green and Brent's cap is yellow. They both wear sunglasses.

Two extremely obese Beagles lie at the feet of Richard and Brent. They are panting heavily now, even before the rabbit hunt begins, because the journey from where Richard and Brent parked their pickup has taken its toll.

"How long's it been since those dogs been run?" Mr. Downs asks in a deep tone.

"About a year," Richard answers.

"Looks like they eatin' good," Mr. Thomas observes, also in a deep tone.

"They eat better than we do," Brent says.

The dogs pay no attention to this conversation. They stretch out on their sides and doze off. They would prefer to remain here most of the day.

Mr. Downs perks upward in his saddle and looks along the winding road leading to his stable from the highway. "Wonder who that could be?" he asks.

The others glance in the same direction and observe a boy of probably 12 years walking very slowly toward them. The boy wears cutoff blue jean shorts and a t-shirt, which is quite courageous considering the temperature reads about 55 degrees.

"Never seen him around here before," Mr. Downs says.

"You think he's here for the hunt?" Mr. Thomas asks.

"Don't have a gun," Richard says.

"Looks lost to me," Brent says.

When the boy finally reaches the crew he smiles broadly and waves. His eyes bulge and a thick purple vein wiggles down the middle of his forehead. He's a lanky, wirey lad. He wears high-top tennis shoes.

"Looks like I at the right place," he says.

The others glance at each other and shrug.

"You come for the rabbit hunt?" Mr. Downs asks.

"Yessuh."

"Well how exactly do you intend on killin' those rabbits?" Mr. Downs asks.

"You mean cause I ain't got no gun," the boy states, his shoulders bobbing with his chuckles. "See suh, I don't use no gun. I don't need one 'cause I don't kill no rabbits. I jump 'em."

"You jump 'em?" Mr. Thomas questions.

"Yessuh. I jump 'em. I go in the weeds and jump 'em and then you shoot 'em."

Mr. Downs and Mr. Thomas break into loud laughter. Richard and Brent squint at the boy. Dog 1 and Dog 2 stir a little.

"I jump 'em all the time for my old man," the boy says.

"Who is your old man?" Mr. Downs asks.

"Mr. Rowdy Brooks, suh."

"Y'all live near here?" Mr. Thomas asks.

"About five miles from here, on the other side of town," the boy replies.

"What's your name, boy?" Mr. Downs asks.

"Little Rowdy."

"So you say you can jump rabbits?" Mr. Thomas questions.

"Yessuh. I know I can jump 'em a lot better than these fat ole dogs."

"Watch your mouth, boy," Richard says.

"I can jump three rabbits 'for these mutts even stand up," Little Rowdy declares.

"I tell you to hush up," Richard warns, "'fore I be jumping on you with yo' braggin' self."

"You better listen to my friend here," Brent adds, tapping his shotgun on his boot.

Dog 1 and Dog 2 stand. They sense they're being ridiculed.

"Now everybody hold on a second," Mr. Thomas says, grinning at Mr. Downs. "Tell me, Mr. Downs, if you had to choose would you say these two dogs or Little Rowdy could jump more rabbits in the next two hours?"

Mr. Downs chuckles and pulls at his earlobe, realizing what Mr. Thomas has in mind.

"Tell you the truth, Mr. Thomas, in all my years of huntin' I never seen a boy who could jump rabbits. I never even heard of it."

"That makes two of us," Mr. Thomas says.

"Then again, I ain't ever seen two rabbit dogs quite like Dog 1 and Dog 2 either," Mr. Downs adds.

"These dogs'll double what this crazy boy jumps, if he can jump 'em at all," Richard says. "Frankly I think he's full of it."

"These dogs'll spook three times more rabbits than this boy," Brent assures.

"H-m-m-m," Mr. Downs breathes as he studies Little Rowdy and the dogs. "I have to go with the dogs. I just can't picture the boy doin' it. Guess I'm too much of a traditionalist when it comes to these types of things."

Mr. Thomas tugs his beard. He looks the boy over real good. "I'd be willin' to wager on the boy," he says. "Don't ask me why."

"Richard, Brent, Little Rowdy, y'all head into the field with the dogs," Mr. Downs instructs. "The patch over by Gunter's creek's a good place to start. Me and Mr. Thomas will be along. We got some discussin' to do."

The trio and the dogs move on with Little Rowdy walking several paces behind. Mr. Downs turns to Mr. Thomas. "How much?"

"You seem pretty sure of yourself," Mr. Thomas says.

"You was the one wanted to make a contest out of it," Mr. Downs says. "I must admit it does add some excitement to what was gonna be a fairly dull afternoon."

"A thousand dollars on a boy and two dogs?" Mr. Downs questions.

"Is it a bet?" Mr. Thomas asks.

"You're on," Mr. Downs says.

The men shake and ride out to the field to catch up with the others. They stand twenty yards from the brush surrounding the creek.

"When I say go, the hunt begins," Mr. Downs says. "Give a little holler when you jump a rabbit so there won't be no mistaken who saw it first. Are y'all ready?"

Richard and Brent kneel and pat their dogs on the head. They look up and nod. Little Rowdy sticks up his thumb and grins.

"Go!"

The group charges toward the creek bank. The dogs and the boy ramble through the thickets for a good 20 minutes with neither jumping a rabbit.

"Starting to look like we both lose," Mr. Downs says. "Look yonder," Mr. Thomas says.

Little Rowdy hustles about the bush. "There's one!" he shouts. A rabbit zig-zags across the pasture. Mr. Thomas aims and shoots it dead. "Nice goin', Little Rowdy," he hollers.

"You fellas get those dogs moving," Mr. Downs orders.

Suddenly Dog 1 and Dog 2 growl and bury their noses in the weeds. "I think they're on one," Richard says.

Note quite. Dog 1 dashes out of the brush and into the field with a large stick in its mouth. Dog 2 is in hot pursuit.

"Jesus," Mr. Downs says.

Richard and Brent holler the dogs over and give each one a kick. The hounds whimper their way back into the hunt.

"There goes number two!" Little Rowdy calls. Another rabbit emerges and veers toward the horses. Mr. Downs cuts it down as it turns to sprint back into the cluster.

"I don't believe what I'm seein'," Mr. Downs says. "Damn boy must be part dog."

"Too bad those dogs don't have more boy in 'em," laughs Mr. Thomas.

"Let's move to the patch of trees at the end of the creek," Mr. Downs suggests.

Along the way Little Rowdy jumps another rabbit. It springs into the open. "I got her," Mr. Thomas says, firing. The rabbit falls. "That makes three to zero," Mr. Thomas says, trying to hold his merriment.

Meanwhile, Richard and Brent have begun a shouting match with each accusing the other's dog of getting in the way.

"You want me to shoot that dog?" Richard hollers.

"You want me to shoot you?" Brent counters.

"I believe the pressure is getting to your team, Mr. Downs," Mr. Thomas says.

As soon as they reach the next site two large doe fling out of their bed and dart across the field.

"Oh shit," say Richard and Brent.

"Oh shit," says Mr. Downs.

Dog 1 and Dog 2 take off after the deer. The men watch for several minutes until the dogs are out of sight and their yelps fade into the adjacent community.

"Number four comin' at yuh!" Little Rowdy announces from his hands and knees as he crawls out from under a bush. A fat one runs a wide circle around Richard and Brent. They shoot angrily and miss. The rabbit vanishes into the weeds.

"Shall we conclude this affair?" Mr. Thomas offers.

"I need a bourbon and water," Mr. Downs says.

Later, after they've had a couple of drinks and laughed about the day's spectacle, and after Mr. Downs has paid Mr. Thomas ten one-hundred dollar bills, Mr. Thomas steers his pickup along the driveway and encounters Little Rowdy sitting against a fence at the turn onto the highway. Mr. Thomas pulls off and nods the boy over.

"That was a thing of beauty you did out there today," Mr. Thomas says, his face gleaming with good fortune. "Mr. Downs don't suspect a thing neither. Why I been wantin' to pull a fast one on that sucker ever since we went to that quail hunt several winters back."

"What happened at the quail hunt, suh?" Little Rowdy asks.

"When we got to the plantation my gun wasn't in the trunk." Mr. Thomas recalls. "And I distinctly remembered putting it there. I had to tell the best quail shooters in the deep South that I'd left my gun at home. Talk about an embarrassin' situation. Mr. Downs finally owned up to it about three years later. Said he had an itchin' to take that gun out right before we left."

"I think you got him back real good today," Little Rowdy says, squeaking laughter.

Mr. Thomas opens his wallet and removes one of the hundred dollar bills. "Now you be sure and take this back to your daddy, Little Rowdy. Tell him I appreciate him lettin' me take advantage of your fine services."

"This is what you call easy money," Little Rowdy says, snatching the bill.

"That's what you call it," Mr. Thomas says. "Course, I aim to give it back, in about three years."

"You and my daddy gonna go huntin' anytime soon?" Little Rowdy asks.

"Tell him I'll be givin' him a call, boy."

Mr. Thomas watches the boy run off. He starts his truck and then sits back with a quick thought: "I wonder if Little Rowdy is any good with quail?"

Kelly is quite obliging to talk turkey in his pleasant home near
the Mobile Bay as he puffs on a pipe and pats his Springer Spaniel
named Freckles. Kelly's voice is deep with a slight coarseness to it.
He has a tendency to cuss and laugh a lot. He began writing in 1973
when his wife, Ellen, suggested he write down some of the stories he had
been telling for years.

Kelly stops short of calling himself a professional writer, noting that he
doesn't have to write for bread and meat, and thus doesn't have to rewrite
his material upon an editor's whim. He recalls writing a piece about a
dove shoot involving himself and his little girl and then being informed by
the outdoor magazine editor that stories with girls in it simply didn't
sell. The editor asked Kelly to change the girl to a boy. He refused and
prevailed.

"Turkey huntin' is the closest thing to an intellectual exercise of any thing I know," he says. "I think you could do it for 80 years and the last year, the last day you'd learn something. It is a constant search for individual pieces of intelligence. You gotta make a series of tactical decisions and invariably when you are wrong you were wrong 30 minutes ago; you realize it and there ain't a damn thing you can do about it. You wash that out and try again."

Kelly credits a declining rural population and stricter adherence to game laws as key reasons for the surge of the turkey population in the past 30 years. "Until the 1950s there weren't enough turkeys in this state to count," he says. "You'd go into a town like Monroeville or Greenville and there might be four or five old crocks in there that hunted turkey and that's all. Then some time just along about then in the 50s all of a sudden people begin to find turkeys. One reason was the lack of rural population, fewer guys livin' out there and feedin' their families on turkeys and turkey eggs and killing turkeys in August. And then too beginnin' about then violation of game laws became not socially acceptable. You know when Alabama first had game wardens they were called possum sheriffs. And it was a term of degradation. You showed your manhood by killing 10 times over the limit. I think game law violation is no longer fashionable."

Kelly compares the turkey hunter to a chess player, or the guy who likes a 1-0 baseball game instead of a 13-12 game. "The hammer is always hanging over your head," he says. "It's three hours of complete, slow, drag-ass boredom and then 15 seconds of extremely quick action. Because it's so slow and difficult, I don't think it's ever going to be as popular as deer hunting. We live in a success-oriented society. When you take a guy huntin' the more rank he's got the more important it is that he kill something. But turkeys don't understand that. They don't give a damn if you've got the chief executive officer down there. They're gonna embarrass him just as badly as they would if you invited the plumber. It's just too damn slow. People wanna shoot the gun, hear the noise, smell the smoke and pile things up in piles."

About two weeks before deer season opens, Fears relaxes in one of his three lodges. He wears a cap over thinning hair and sports a ruffled reddish beard. His eyes barely squint as he speaks. He looks a decade younger then his age of 46.

"When I'm in Alaska I'll have a hunter fly in from the Southeast and one from a New England state," says Fears, who has guided expeditions worldwide. "I find the Southern hunter is willing to push a little harder, willing to climb a little steeper mountain. The deep South hasn't been too many years ago from being an agrarian society, so we still have a lot of good ole boys runnin' around here that aren't but one generation removed from the land. You can see that in their hunting."

When acting as a guide Fears makes it his business before the hunt
to see what kind of people he's working with. He leads them to the rifle
range so that they can check their scopes which may have been
knocked off during their travels. That's what he tells them anyway. What he
is really doing is watching how they handle their guns and themselves. He doesn't need too many minutes to know if they grew up on a
farm or in downtown Boston, especially if they show up not knowing
how to shoot, or with a rifle of one caliber and shells of another. Fears says
he's relieved when an ole farm boy arrives, because he won't have to
worry about that farm boy shooting anybody accidentally or getting lost at
the end of the afternoon hunt. "Some of these other dudes bring a
compass with 'em and they've never taken the time to learn how to use it,"
he says. "Some of 'em are absolutely terrified when we pick them up
at night. They shoot every round they have at noises in the dark. The good
ole boy's a little more polished. He's killed some animals growing up."

Wayne Fears may have hunted everything everywhere, but he's still just a good ole boy who likes to get out in the woods. "I don't have to kill anything," he says. "I've taken my share of nice animals. I enjoy squirrel huntin' as much as I do climbin' any mountain in Alaska after a dolar sheep. I can get down here in one of these creek bottoms with a .22 rifle, spend the day squirrel huntin' and I've had a ball, even if I don't kill a squirrel. It's the opportunity to be alone, no deadlines, just the sites and smells and the fact that I can sit there and not feel guilty about not doing a damn thing. To me that's what hunting is all about. These people that are compelled to kill and put big heads on the wall, they're missing something. They're flat missing something."

But isn't the kill the main reason hunters hunt? Fears doesn't believe so. In fact he places it way down the totem pole. More important, he says, is the chance to get outdoors, to understand and practice the skills associated with hunting, to learn more about the animals themselves (he calls hunters amateur naturalists), to travel and get away for the weekend whether to a house in the woods that's an old battered tenant shack or a plush accommodation like Fears' lodge, to live an alternate lifestyle, to experience the comradery, to maintain some touch with fading rural society.

And then, only then, comes the kill.